Dog Tales

Heart-warming tales of rescue
dogs who rescued their
owners right back

Andrea Hayes

Gill Books

Gill Books
Hume Avenue
Park West
Dublin 12
www.gillbooks.ie
Gill Books is an imprint of M.H. Gill and Co.

Design and print origination by O'K Graphic Design, Dublin
Edited by Rachel Pierce
Printed by CPI Group (UK) Ltd, Croydon CRO 4YY
This book is typeset in 12/18 pt Bembo.

All photographs courtesy of Dogs Trust except for the below.
p. 2 © TV3
p. 31 © Jenny McCarthy
p. 115 © Marc O'Sullivan
p. 209 © *Irish Daily Mail*
pp. 56, 72, 90, 120, 159 © Fran Veale
p. 299 © Michael Chester

The paper used in this book comes from the wood pulp of managed forests. For every tree felled, at least one tree is planted, thereby renewing natural resources.

A CIP catalogue record for this book is available from the British Library.

5 4 3 2 1

For Dad

Contents

Foreword by Clarissa Baldwin

Andrea Hayes' wonderfully charming book is an absolute must for all dog lovers. I defy your heart not to melt when reading each of these dogs' tales.

In 1978, I was tasked by Dogs Trust (then called National Canine Defence League) to come up with a slogan that encompassed all that the charity was trying to achieve. At a time when the charity had very little money, the slogan had to be memorable and used in a format that cost very little money. 'A Dog is for Life Not Just for Christmas' was selected, and it has become an iconic slogan which has stood the test of time. Of course, it is disappointing that the message has to be constantly reinforced and I still look forward to the day when it is no longer necessary. However, I fear that the day when everybody understands the full responsibilities of dog ownership is still some way off.

In my four decades with Dogs Trust I have seen the charity grow from a small-scale organisation to one that is thriving, enabling us to rescue over 15,000 dogs a year. The charity is also active in nearly forty countries around the world, teaching responsible dog ownership and supporting charities in their dog management work.

On the whole, as a society we love dogs, but there is a small minority who are extraordinarily cruel. When a dog comes into the charity in a terrible state, either mentally or physically, and, after a huge amount of dedicated work and care from the team, goes to a new home, it is a very happy moment and a time to celebrate.

This book captures the incredible stories of thirteen dogs and their journeys through this period of their life. It highlights the huge amount of work that goes into returning a dog to a happy, healthy state, so praise for the staff involved can not be overemphasised.

In a very moving way, Andrea captures how rescue dogs can change your life just as much as you might change theirs. Take, for instance, the story of Jano, a dog with a broken back who was rescued by a lady with a broken spirit. She had no intention of adopting a dog that day, but fell in love with little Jano. In truth, Jano rescued his new owner.

I do hope you will enjoy this wonderful book as much as I have.

Clarissa Baldwin CBE
Former CEO of Dogs Trust
Dogs Trust Trustee

A message from Suzie Carley

From all of us in Dogs Trust, but most especially from all the dogs we have helped in the past, those currently in our care and for those who will need us in the future, thank you for buying this book. In doing so you are helping to give a rescue dog a second chance in life.

As you will read, Andrea's story in animal welfare began in 2005, as did our work in Ireland by educating young children in primary schools about the responsibilities of dog ownership. In 2009, we opened our state-of-the-art rehoming centre in Finglas, Dublin. Today, we are Ireland's largest dog welfare charity, caring for over 2,500 dogs and puppies a year – wonderful dogs like Penny, Claude, Alex, Kelly and my little foster puppy 'Bumpy', whose inspiring and heartwarming stories you are about to read in this book.

The strength of our work and the impact it has made in dog welfare in this country over the past twelve years is down to the dedication, care and professionalism of our wonderful supporters, staff and volunteers. Stories of these lives are beautifully captured and told through the eyes of our newest volunteer canine carer, Andrea Hayes.

As you turn the pages in this book, you will see for yourself how the bond between humans and dogs is something so unique and very special – and something that we will continue to fight for. Our mission is to bring about a day when all dogs can enjoy a happy life, free from the threat of unnecessary destruction.

So from all at Dogs Trust Ireland, thank you from the bottom of our hearts. Enjoy our *Dog Tales*.

Suzie Carley
Executive Director
Dogs Trust Ireland

PART 1

My Life with Dogs

Dash and Andrea (2009)

A person who has never owned a dog has missed a wonderful part of life.

BOB BARKER

2005: A broken heart

In April 2005 my father passed away and I was completely broken-hearted. My pain was so deep, I felt I might never be the same person again. I felt I had lost a part of me, I felt alone and frightened, my champion was gone and I felt truly hopeless. He had battled cancer for over a year, but in the end, the strongest man in my life became weaker and weaker and finally drifted away from us and passed on from this life.

The months that followed were almost a blur. I was overwhelmed by a tumultuous wave of emotions. I was at sea and not myself in any way. At the time, I couldn't think of Dad without crying. When I returned to work, I had to make a determined effort not to well up when colleagues offered condolences. But eventually it all became too much and by the end of the summer I decided to leave a job that I loved to explore working freelance.

Society often writes off the death of a parent as the natural order of events, but for me it was completely life-changing. My grief created an awareness of life that I had never experienced before. I suddenly had a lot of time on my hands, and I started to look at my own life and health. I realised that I needed to look after myself better.

I have a well-documented history of living with a chronic illness, but until that point I hadn't properly explored what was really going in internally with my own body. As my grief and pain were so apparent, my doctors were quick to suggest I needed antidepressants. I took them for a short while, but I knew my pain was something deeper.

The new year of 2006 ushered in a new chapter for me. I knew in my heart that I needed to find joy in my life again. The feelings of hurt and loss still filled my head, but my heart was stronger than I could have ever imagined.

2006: Dashy Dog and Me

A special four-legged Valentine's Day arrival made my heart grow in love and confidence and beat with new hope.

David and I had been together for almost eight years and he had been my rock through my Dad's illness and the dark months that followed his death. We had recently got engaged, and our plans for the future were firmly set in stone. Every day I was feeling a little bit brighter and, luckily for me, the love and support of David kept me strong. I was also surrounded by wonderful friends, who encouraged me to get out and about.

I began meeting a friend for regular walks on a local beach with her dog, Boo, and we would often chat about our mutual love of animals. One day she mentioned that a lady she knew had a litter of pups and was looking for good homes for them. She showed me a picture of the mum, who was a Labrador Retriever with lovely shiny golden hair. She told me the owner had successfully found homes for a few of the puppies, but still needed to rehome the rest. I can't explain it, but instantly I felt I needed to rehome one of those dogs.

Later that day I contacted the owner and we spoke at length. She wanted to ensure that any new owners would be suitable, but she immediately seemed happy with our circumstances. I wasn't working full-time, so I could be there during the day for a new puppy, and this was really important for her. However, David and I hadn't any shared experience caring for a dog. She asked me about 'my situation'. I told her we had our own house and were engaged to be married. I explained that the dog would be part of the family and that, for me, it would be the biggest commitment we had ever made; houses can be sold, but caring for a dog is for life!

I passed the test, thankfully, and the owner felt happy to let us have one of the pups. We agreed a date for us to collect him, and it happened to be 14 February – Valentine's Day. What a perfect day to start a new love affair! We drove for a long time through terrible rain, but at last we found the house. Once inside, we met the mum and dad and their boisterous bunch of puppies, all scrabbling for attention.

I will never forget walking into this stranger's home and seeing a larger, shy golden ball of fluff hiding behind his brothers and sisters. This particular pup seemed quieter and less confident than the rest. David reached in and picked him up, and he cuddled into David's chest as if it was the home he'd always been waiting for. Ever since then, and for evermore, his paw-print is on our hearts and lives.

Leaving behind his mother, littermates, first human family and the only small part of the world he had ever seen was monumental for our little puppy, and he wouldn't leave David's chest for a second. So I took over the driving, taking us quietly and carefully back along the roads we had come by, bringing the newest member of our clan home.

Relocating to a new home is a major day in a puppy's life, but really, it was a huge day for all of us, not least me. After all the excitement, stress, massive change and huge amount of mental stimulation our new little puppy had just been through, he needed to sleep. Soon after arriving home we placed him in his new bed and he put his head on his paws, closed his eyes and drifted off. We just couldn't help staring at him.

We knew our lives had changed forever when we woke a few hours later to little cries and whines from downstairs. The enormity of caring for a puppy soon became crystal clear. It was a sleepless night for us, but when morning came our frightened little puppy seemed to have found his footing. He ran around the house like a hurricane, sniffing his way through every nook and cranny, sticking his nose into absolutely everything, bouncing up and down and in and out of every place imaginable. He couldn't stay still, dashing off to the next adventure whenever I tried to get him to sit down. We decided to call him Dash.

Our new four-legged friend eventually stopped and rested in the corner, silently appraising his new parents and watching the world around him, almost afraid to close his eyes in case he might miss something. It was amazing how quickly he became part of our home – it was hard to remember what it was like before his arrival. With Dash, there was a sense of belonging from day one.

In the days and weeks that followed, Dash settled in and we really started to see his true personality shine through. Just like me, Dash has a penchant for nice shoes, as I discovered one Sunday morning when he decided to raid my wardrobe. Puppies explore the world with their mouths, so after Dash had had a good chew, he proudly delivered his work to me – much to my distress! That was an important lesson on the consequences of leaving Dash to roam free in our home of a Sunday morning when I fancied an extra-long lie-in – walls, furniture, shoes; they were all fair game for him to chew on.

To avoid another shoe-gate, or chew-gate, I became obsessed with finding the perfect chew toys. In the end, it was something simple that worked the best: Dash got endless hours of joy from an empty plastic bottle. We spent hours throwing bottles instead of balls, and our new fur baby just loved to have fun retrieving them and then cleverly chewing the lid off and presenting it to us.

We all settled into our new routine, and I really enjoyed watching him learn. I had a rigid schedule for feeding, playing and potty breaks, so it was only a matter of weeks before Dash was fully house-trained.

From the moment Dash came into our lives he enjoyed spending time outdoors, whether it was running around with his four-legged pals at the beach or taking a hike with us into the mountains, he just loved getting out, and that got me out too. I got so much pleasure watching him explore, and he became the joy I had been missing in my life. With Dash by my side, I had a new spring in my step.

They say time is a great healer for grief, but so is a dog. By opening my heart to Dash, I slowly started to heal from the loss of Dad and accept my new reality. I used to joke and say my dad had sent Dash to me, as a cure to heal the pain of loss. Dash's medicine is fierce loyalty, reliability, nobleness, trustworthiness, unconditional love, friendship, and endless energy for service. From him I have learned the true meaning of unconditional love.

Dash is so sensitive and intelligent; he's the perfect companion. Over time our bond grew and grew and he seemed to be my protector, always by my side and always close by when I needed him. I began to believe he could almost read my mind! I felt he knew what I was thinking.

One example of this springs to mind. I can often struggle when carrying things and, like most people, I sometimes carry too many things at once. However, due to muscle weakness in my arms and hands from my chronic pain condition, I often drop things, and juggling to open doors when your hands are full isn't always a good idea. So one day, quite by surprise, Dash jumped up and with his paws managed to press the door handle down and it opened for me! I was actually dumb-struck, because in my mind I had been thinking: I wish the door was open.

If you own a dog, you will know that they are constantly observing you. I wondered if Dash could anticipate my next move.

They say a dog's behaviour often mirrors the personality of its owner, so I began to explore how to train a Labrador. Armed with my new knowledge, our training began. It was new territory for both of us, so we started with the basics. I wanted to see if I could teach him to open more doors for me, maybe even the front door? Perhaps he could help me around the house.

Training and bonding with Dash ultimately helped me more than it did Dash. While I was teaching him tricks and ways to improve his behaviour, it helped me to assess my own situation and to realise that with him around, I felt safer. Feeling safe is an important part of growing as a person and feeling joyful, and I realised that this was Dash's gift to me. Through our carefully planned daily routine, which we stuck to whatever the weather, I had a reason to get up in the morning and a focus to every part of my day. I was engaging with the world again, chatting to fellow dog owners on our walks, planning outings, thinking ahead. I suddenly realised I was looking forward to the future. The training required dedication on my part, and was challenging, but through it I learned to be more patient, to show more empathy, to be more loving and considerate, to let things go, to control my temper more effectively and, most of all, to enjoy the moment and to be organised and disciplined. It turned out to be the best antidepressant anyone could have prescribed.

Florence Nightingale, a pioneer of modern nursing, once wrote that a pet 'is often an excellent companion for the sick, for long, chronic cases especially'. In my case, I can tell you this is perfectly true. Privately, I was struggling with my health issues and although many people would never see me battle with the pain, Dash, my faithful companion and constant support, saw everything – the good days and the bad. He was there when no one else was. He was always with me, one hundred percent reliable.

I remember how he would often encourage me out of bed, even if I was feeling terrible. When he rested his face softly on my shoulder or leg, I couldn't resist his pleading expression. He seemed to know that I needed extra comfort and love when I was feeling low.

Most pet owners can tell you of a time when a loyal pet lay by their side, attentive and patient, while they were in bed with the flu. Dash seemed to do this daily for me. He offered me immense comfort and because he was so undemanding, I felt safe with him. He would see me cry in pain and would instantly know I needed to snuggle up with him. We had a bond of absolute trust. He became my counsellor with fur, and I would often open up to him about my health fears. He was a great confidant, never judging and ever listening.

Dash became a central part of my journey to wellness. I feel so grateful that he came into my life. He is an amazingly gentle, caring soul who offers me so much comfort and love and I honestly can say that he has changed my life.

When I was exploring the many ways to heal from my own chronic pain, I came across a lot of studies on how just petting an animal can make humans feel better. We all know the canine bond goes back thousands of years, ever since humans and wolf dogs lived in settlements, but now science and research have revealed that petting your dog releases oxytocin, which is a hormone associated with bonding and affection in both humans and dogs. Oxytocin promotes love and trust (which is why it is a key hormone released during childbirth) and is linked to reduced blood pressure and heart rate. So by simply reaching out to your dog, you will experience lower blood pressure and reduced anxiety – simply from sharing your life with a dog.

On a chemical level, owning a pet may also decrease levels of cortisol (a stress hormone that can damage your body) in your blood, and raise levels of the feel-good brain chemical dopamine. This means you will feel better emotionally, feeling happier and more positive. I certainly felt these effects in my own life. Just knowing Dash was around and knowing I wasn't alone with my pain had a profoundly positive effect on me.

All the while I was engaging with the medical professions and after exploring many options for treatment for chronic pain I was advised to try a pain management course. I signed up for a three-week full-time course in St Vincent's Hospital in Dublin, and after completing it I was in a really good place. Dash was at the heart of what I was trying to achieve. I actually wrote him into my pain management home plan, as undertaking to take him – and myself – for a walk every single day. Previously I had often gone on hikes or walks with him that were totally unsuitable because I pushed too hard and for too long, which wasn't helpful. Now I identified two suitable walks: a shorter twenty-five-minute one, and a longer forty-five-minute one. They became the paths I plodded daily, with my loyal friend by my side.

I had an incredible feeling of gratitude for my four-legged angel. I knew he was there to watch over me. In truth, he was the love of my life, he was just so kind, loyal and forever loving. I had fallen head over heels in love with Dash, and I wanted to keep him happy, safe and healthy. When he was happy, I was happy too. Dash gave me the joy I had lost in my life. And as the old saying goes, what you focus on expands. Now that I was happier in myself, I was ready to start living again and embrace new challenges. Dash had prepared me re-enter my own life and he was changing too as he settled into his older more relaxed adult dog years.

2009: Auditions and Audacious Actions

In a happier place in my life both physically and mentally, I was ready to embrace the unexpected and my love for Dash would be central to making a change in direction career-wise. I had been working for TV3 for four years, presenting station announcements (continuity). Getting work as a television presenter can be very difficult as there are so many people interested in doing it and not a lot of roles. It had never really been a strong desire of mine to work in front of the camera, as my skills had always been utilised behind the scenes. But after two successful years presenting daytime continuity with one of my human best friends, Conor Clear, our TV gig was coming to an end. My future in TV presenting was uncertain, but I was pretty sure I would only do something I was really passionate about.

As it happened, I wasn't waiting long before I heard of a job that seemed the perfect fit for me. It involved presenting a new show, which would be far more demanding than the presenting I had done up to that point. The only obstacle now was getting it. Many people were being seen for the role, so I would have to perform strongly in the interviews and audition.

The screen test for the programme was different from anything I had ever experienced before. I was asked to show up at a vet's office at an allocated time – and that's all I was told. Normally for TV auditions, first impressions matter hugely. Your appearance, training and skills are all in the spotlight, so when the cameras start to roll, it can be a very nervous and overwhelming experience. But something felt different that day. I was strangely calm about it. I had a feeling that all I had to do to land the job was to be myself. I just knew, deep down, that I would be right for the job, despite having little to no actual experience working with animals. I was so convinced this job was perfect for me and me for it that I did little to prepare. I hadn't even worn much make-up or dressed up for my moment to impress. I was hoping I would impress the real stars of the show – the animals I was about to meet.

I walked into the 'audition' and was asked to interview the vet on the animal I was handed, which happened to be a cute and rather spritely mixed-fur ferret. I didn't know much about handling these little creatures, so I wasn't expecting the very friendly and inquisitive little guy to quickly scamper from out of my arms to all around my neck. It was clear the ferret was bright and alert, so I was interested to find out why he was visiting the vet. Luckily, it was a routine visit.

I was so engaged with the brilliant vet, Barbara O'Malley, that I quickly forgot about the cameras, and they just kept rolling. We chatted about his care, diet and lifespan. It felt quite natural, despite the crew around, and we spoke very happily for the next ten minutes. Then we decided our little furry friend would get his nails clipped, and naturally my instinct was to help Barbara and keep him distracted while she got the job done. I felt I didn't do anything special during the visit, and I wasn't sure if I was saying what the producers were looking for, but I had thoroughly enjoyed myself anyway.

The news was good. In 2009 I was offered a presenting job on a new show for TV3 called *Animal A&E*. To my surprise, there were to be two presenters, Michael Hayes and myself. He would be on location working with vets, while my role was as a roving reporter, working on stories around the country. The person at the helm of programming in TV3, Ben Frow, really championed the idea of highlighting the work of animal welfare organisations around Ireland. It was agreed I would do a weekly 'report' on this work. My director, Andrew Byrne, and I discussed it in more detail and we looked at linking in with the ISPCA in order to highlight the suffering of animals nationwide.

Although I had never worked in the area of animal welfare in any way, it felt familiar to me. My own day-to-day suffering often goes unnoticed, and somehow that made me feel connected to the animals who were suffering silent abuse, locked away from help, at the mercy of an uncaring owner. I felt a surge of determination. I wanted to work hard to bring attention to any animals in pain. This outpouring of emotion and desire to help surprised me, but it was like, having battled my own pain, I was finally being given a chance to make a difference and help others who were suffering. It lit a fire inside me that's burning still.

So that's how it all started. After all those years at home with Dash, spending so much time alone and feeling bowed down by grief and pain, now I began travelling the country and working on a job that I truly loved. It was a huge turnaround for me personally, and I was so grateful for it. The presenting role was a challenge on so many different levels, physically and emotionally, but I relished it. I was afforded wonderful opportunities to work closely with people who were involved in the rescue, rehabilitation and rehoming of all kinds of animals every year. I interacted with hundreds of sick and injured animals all over the country and seen amazing stories of survival and kindness that I will never forget. Sometimes, I felt like I had witnessed miracles.

Filming the welfare work being carried out around Ireland was uplifting and terribly difficult all at once. The vast majority of the animals I met were often terrified of human contact, not surprising given that many had been treated in an appalling manner by the ones they loyally loved and in whom they placed their trust. An animal's strongest instinct is to survive – that fight or flight reaction – and self-preservation will always kick in when they are most in need. Sometimes even getting 'hands on' with these sick, needy animals just isn't possible. It requires a massive amount of patience to build up trust, but of course time wasn't always on my side when working within the parameters of a film shoot. I always wondered how the animals I met along the way were doing after being rescued, and I often tried to stay in touch with their carers or new owners. I had no idea then that my desire to find out the end of these animals' stories would propel me in a new and exciting direction.

2011: A Growing Family

David, Dash and I made a lovely trio, we did everything together and loved sharing our lives. But after almost seven years of being parents to Dash alone, I became pregnant. Our family dynamic was about to change again.

Becoming pregnant was a big dream of mine, but until it happened I wasn't sure if it ever would. My health issues were a big factor, so it took a lot of preparation to reduce my medication to be able to conceive safely. So when it finally happened, it was such a blessing. However, the pregnancy, and later the birth, didn't come without their own challenges. I had to spend a lot of time in bed and resting. But I was never alone – my 'shadow', as David often referred to Dash, was always beside me, and he was there as we prepared to meet our new daughter.

While we were planning my hospital bag, the colour of the baby's room and picking out the perfect travel system for our new arrival, we didn't overlook our first, four-legged baby. Although my 'to do' list seemed endless, I knew Dash was very sensitive to changes in his routine and surroundings, including the new sights and smells of all the baby things that were now taking up space in the house. We were careful not to leave Dash out of the preparations, and his care was planned just as carefully and comprehensively.

In the weeks before my due date, Dash and I enrolled for boot-camp training. He was now fully grown, but we had both let the obedience training slip a little and I wanted to address some niggling concerns I had about the bad habits we had all allowed to go on. I remember at the time that what had seemed like minor concerns until now, such as jumping up on the couch or on guests, suddenly seemed significant. We wanted everything in the household working in harmony when the baby arrived. We had also allowed him into our room to sleep, and I really wanted to adjust that and reintroduce him to his own sleeping space and new, comfy bed so he would be settled into this new routine before the big arrival.

We decided it was best to nip any behavioural issues in the bud, which is why we went to boot camp. This, in fact, brought us even closer as I was working with Dash every day. It reminded me of when he was a puppy, and we were getting to know each other and working out a new routine. It was the first time I had stopped to think: our little puppy is all grown up.

Once I had the house ready and Dash's manners in check, I needed to give Dash a complete health-check with the vet and some TLC with the groomers before baby arrived. He got a clean bill of health from the vet, who told us he was in tip-top shape, and his 'pet-icure' ensured his nails were short, to avoid any accidental scratches!

I remember thinking that everything would be different once the newest member of the family arrived. If I am honest, I was concerned that having a baby might have a bad effect on Dash, with possibly serious consequences if he failed to adapt to having a baby in his environment.

Luckily, I had nothing to worry about. Dash was as loving and protective over the baby as he was with me.

The night before she arrived, I was in her room checking that everything was in place and Dash, as always, was by my side. I remember letting him sniff some of the baby wipes, nappies and her newborn clothes, talking to him and telling him that soon we would have a little baby to care for. He seemed to be the one calming me down with a loving nudge and nuzzle, as if telling me it would be okay. And it was.

Our gorgeous daughter, Brooke, was born at 6.05 p.m. on 12 July 2011. While we were still in the hospital, David brought home an outfit Brooke had worn so Dash could get used to her smell. We had planned to have Dash at my mother-in-law's house on the day Brooke and I came home, so we could get settled before the meet and greet, but life doesn't always go as planned. We were so happy to get the baby into the car seat, navigate the roads of Dublin, avoiding the bumps on the road, that when we arrived at the front door we remembered Dash was still at home! As expected, the initial face-to-face meeting was more about him saying hi to me than to the baby. He was so eager to see his mummy again that at first he barely noticed a very proud daddy holding our bundle of joy.

To mark the special day, we had a nice chewy bone ready for Dash to play with, and he took it joyfully. After a while he sniffed around Brooke, he was very curious about her for the first hour, but then he went to his bed and relaxed.

And that was that – he accepted the new housemate and the new living situation from that moment on.

I was so busy in those first few weeks that it was hard to take time out, but I felt I needed time for me and for Dash, so we tried to get out for a little walk every day. I was extra-attentive at bedtime, making sure to give Dash a big belly rub, to let him know he was still important, still loved.

I found positive reinforcement goes a long way, and it smoothed our transition from trio to quartet. A safe household is a happy household, and Dash has now grown up with Brooke and they are the best of pals. Brooke is now big enough to take him for a walk on his lead, with a little supervision, and their bond continues to deepen. Watching our little family grow, and grow together, brings me so much happiness, and watching Dash grow older every year is a reminder of just how important he has been in my life. He serves selflessly, never asking for his service to be praised or anything in return.

Dash remains my constant companion, and he always has a watchful eye on me. His quick thinking helped me once more when David was away on business. It was just after 7.00 a.m. and I was getting up to wake Brooke and get her ready for crèche. There was only the three of us in the house and when the alarm went off, I jumped up as normal. It wouldn't be unusual for me to be a little unsteady on my feet, but on this particular morning something happened that had never happened before. As I walked across the landing into my daughter's room, I collapsed to the ground before even reaching the door and passed out cold in the hallway. I regained consciousness moments later, to a familiar tongue licking me and a familiar nose almost nudging me to become alert. I was still very weak and I was really scared. I actually had no idea what had happened or why. I began to call to Brooke from the hallway to help me, and true to form my daughter didn't want to get out of bed. Despite lots of calling and coaxing, I couldn't get her out to the hallway to help me. Luckily, Dash seemed to instantly know I needed him to do something. He began to bark loudly, then ran into her room and barked at her to get her attention, and he did! She reluctantly came out and once she was there, I managed to stand up, but I instantly felt weak again and fell down. Brooke was able to get my phone and bring it to me so I could call for help.

I couldn't seem to stop this feeling of being lightheaded, so I slowly sat up and began crawling back into my bedroom, and Dash, like my true hero, kept willing me along, putting his head under mine. Just having him by my side kept me calm and I felt safer. I felt he understood.

Shortly after that I had a tilt table test in the Mater hospital in Dublin and I was diagnosed with a condition called postural orthostatic tachycardia syndrome (POTS). For a person with POTS, a change from the supine position to an upright position causes an abnormally large increase in heart rate, which can lead to dizziness and, in my case, a fainting episode. This new diagnosis goes some way to explaining why I collapsed and passed out that morning.

Dash is an incredibly smart dog, and I truly believe he has a type of sixth sense when it comes to my health and me. He knew I wasn't well that morning, and understood that I needed help. He sees something that most people don't see when they look at me. I have many chronic conditions – Chiari malformation 1, spinal stenosis, POTS and mild EDS – that all can cause many side effects, not least chronic pain, but sadly they are invisible to most. Dash, however, can read the subtle clues when I am in pain, even when I try to conceal it from him.

I know it's a total cliché and something that has been written about time and time again throughout history about dogs, but it is so true – they truly are guardians, protectors and, most importantly, (wo)man's best friend. Dash is the most loyal companion anyone could ever ask for. My shadow, my joy. And you know, you've probably seen him – perhaps even admired his beauty – because he always makes an appearance in my TV shows, and if you watch carefully, you will see him running in the long grass during the opening titles for the series *Dog Tales*. It's only right, seeing as his part in my life is largely responsible for my career. Without Dash, I wouldn't have had the courage – or the health – to go for that first presenting job. I wouldn't have had such a burning passion to help dogs in need. Dash's love and affection, and the effect that has had on me, inspired me to want to work with animals and to try, in some small way, to make a difference.

2011: The Dark Side of *Dog Tales*

One particularly upsetting rescue operation changed my mindset and will forever stay with me. It had such a profound effect on me that I began to think the problem of animal cruelty was almost insurmountable, and I knew I needed to take more action to change our current, casual view of buying dogs from puppy farms.

Nothing could have prepared me for what I was about to witness in a quiet location in the midlands. I was working with two of the ISPCA inspectors, filming for my first animal show with TV3's *Animal A&E*. We went to a house, following up on an anonymous call about alleged animal cruelty. We arrived at a property on an old country road and to the untrained eye, everything seemed completely normal. I remember there was what appeared to be a happy, healthy small terrier-type dog running around in a garden to the side of the house, and we could visibly see an outside kennel with two bowls – one filled with water and the other seemed to be for food. At that point I was absolutely sure we had arrived at the wrong property or that there was some discrepancy in the allegation of neglect, which had often been the case in the past.

The two ISPCA inspectors went ahead and spoke at length with the owner of the property. While I waited outside, I noticed there was a shed to the rear of the property, but I never for one moment suspected the horror that awaited us inside. I could see the inspectors walking with the owner in the direction of the building. There were no windows in the large stone building, but I noticed a number of makeshift runs on the outside.

Suddenly things began to move very quickly and I was asked to help the team. I was told before I went in that they had grave concerns for the vast number of dogs and puppies inside the huge shed. On first inspection they could clearly see they were living in extremely sub-standard conditions and not receiving the basic care or attention they needed and deserved. I was told the kennels were filthy, wet and overcrowded and that the animals were all very scared, so to proceed with caution.

I braced myself for what I was about to see. The moment I walked in, I was struck by the complete lack of sunlight, and the distinct smell. The crowds of animals huddled together didn't seem to act like dogs, they were almost like robots. I had never seen animals in such bad condition – they were malnourished, sick, with many suffering from advanced chronic skin conditions. I remember the first dog we noticed in grave danger was a Bichon Frise female. She was so weak, and barely moving, clearly in pain and languishing close to death. Sadly, she wasn't the only one. Almost all of the dogs needed urgent medical attention.

We couldn't stay in the building for any great length of time because of the overpowering, unforgettable smell. It was absolutely horrendous. The ammonia in the air made it difficult to breathe. In fact, one of the ISPCA's cameras stopped working because of the extremely dangerous levels of ammonia present from the sheer volume of dog urine soaked into the stone floor of the building.

It was overwhelming, but far from feeling emotional, I seemed to go into action mode. Alongside the ISPCA inspectors, we worked in silence, carefully and slowly assessing the dogs and identifying the most vulnerable, who needed immediate attention. We focused on the work, not really allowing ourselves to stop or think about anything other than getting the animals to safety. More ISPCA staff arrived to help us, and they worked through the night. It was a large-scale operation, which resulted in the safe rescue of well over fifty dogs and puppies. The rescued animals were voluntarily surrendered by the owner and were sent straight to the ISPCA's national animal centre in Longford to receive the treatment, assessment and recuperation they so urgently needed.

I had read about puppy farms, but until I witnessed it first-hand, I could not have comprehended the cruel conditions. The looks on the dogs' faces will haunt me forever – they were petrified. The memory of the trembling, the fear and the guttural growls coming from somewhere deep inside those breeding mums as they tried to keep their young safe, will never leave me. Looking into their eyes changed me forever.

After a few days, I had a chance to see the dogs again in a much safer environment during their vet check at the centre. I was struck by the amount of different breeds rescued – Huskies, West Highland terriers, Jack Russell terriers, Shih Tzus, and, of course, the Bichon Frise. The ISPCA vets also found pregnant bitches and puppies that they aged as just a few days old. Thankfully, all made a full recovery over time and are now rehomed in permanent new homes.

These were the lucky ones, but how many more were suffering in silence around the country? That was the first puppy farm I ever encountered, but sadly, it wasn't to be the last.

The fallout from the rescue operation cost the ISPCA thousands of euro, as all the dogs needed extensive veterinary care. This placed further pressure on the organisation as, like so many other animal charities, they were already struggling to raise funds to look after the animals in their care.

I certainly didn't realise the far-reaching consequences of the problem. Until then, I didn't know that Ireland was known as the puppy farm capital of Europe. I guessed that, like me, many people in Ireland simply had no idea just how cruel the business of puppy farms was. It was a tragedy unfolding right under our noses, but no one seemed to be doing anything about it.

Animal A&E was a family show and we couldn't show some of the footage we had filmed, so to highlight the sheer extent of the problem we went about making a one-hour special called *The Truth about Ireland's Puppy Farms*. This lack of awareness became apparent when this special one-hour documentary was shown on TV3, and our viewers came face-to-face with the bitter reality of the neglect and cruelty suffered by many animals in Ireland. It was deeply moving to watch, and I think it helped bring about change.

The public response to our show was overwhelming. When Irish audiences saw the true reality of this deplorable business, they supported the many welfare charities that were calling on the government to stop this from continuing. The programme really highlighted the urgent need for the incoming Dog Breeding Establishments Bill.

Things did change, and the following January the new Dog Breeding Establishments Bill came into force, which was a step in the right direction. However, without rigorous enforcement of the new Dog Breeding Establishments Act the situation continued and still does to this day.

What people often don't realise is that puppies from puppy farms tend to have physical and behavioural problems as a result of poor breeding. I wanted to help get the message across that people needed to be aware of this, and needed to be extremely selective about from where and from whom they buy a puppy. Most reputable breeders do not sell dogs through newspaper adverts, pet shops, car parks, or through the Internet. Disreputable breeders or middlemen often pose as members of the public selling 'puppies from unplanned litters' in newspaper adverts and online. Sadly, impulse buying of pets online creates an enormous risk of attracting unscrupulous breeders.

My message would always be: adopt, don't shop. It's easy to be taken in, however, and I remember how my own dog, Dash, came into my life. Luckily, I did get to see mother, father and puppy together. It is a hard message, but if you suspect you are purchasing from a puppy farm, don't buy it. Many people think they are saving a dog by doing so, but they are in fact fueling the puppy farm trade to continue their vile so-called business. You can easily call the Dog Warden or the ISPCA and let your concerns be recorded for them to investigate.

Before buying a dog, you need to know that the average dog lives for thirteen years and costs on average €10,000 over its lifetime, depending on the size of the dog. It isn't a decision to be taken lightly or without proper consideration. I have seen the fallout when dogs are discarded and unwanted, and you wouldn't wish that on any animal.

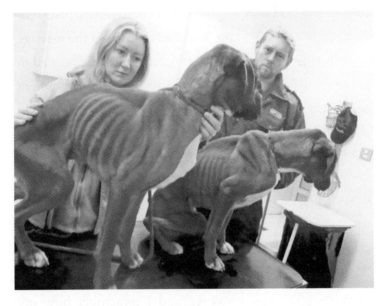

Despite the best-laid plans, life is unpredictable and sometimes bad things happen to good dogs (and their owners). People have to make really tough decisions and sadly, sometimes those include surrendering an animal for their own safety and care. These are often good people in the midst of terrible situations. The act of surrendering and being surrendered is a traumatic experience, and it requires grace and humanity. I have seen understanding and kindness for both parties during my time working with many welfare organisations.

After being in that puppy farm and watching the public reaction to the programme, I knew that the work we were doing was important, necessary and could help bring about change. That made me more determined than ever to do everything possible to make Ireland a safer place for dogs and do my bit to undo the damage brought by greedy, uncaring dog breeders and traders.

2013: Be the change you want to see

As an animal lover, I was appalled by the puppy farm and the fact that it wasn't a one-off was deeply concerning. It's very hard to accept that this is going on all over the country. Filming *Animal A&E* was both uplifting and difficult. What made it uplifting were the humans who dedicated their lives to helping vulnerable animals and, of course, the dogs themselves. It amazed me to discover that even after being abused, neglected, starved and forced into breeding again and again, once rescued and given time and care, these same animals continue to seek human company, attention and affection. They learn to trust again, and usually very quickly. They don't hold on to their terrible experience, but let it go and move on. I found that very inspiring and humbling.

The whole experience changed me and in many ways I was ready to move on, after presenting and associate producing almost sixty episodes of the popular format, which aired across twelve countries, including the USA, Australia, Denmark, Finland, Canada, and on Channel 5 in the UK. Now I wanted to change direction.

I felt a strong desire to create a new show dedicated to the animal who had transformed my life, my loyal dog Dash. The legislation may have changed, but I felt that we, as a nation, needed to educate the next generation to stop the high numbers of unwanted dogs who find themselves in pounds every year.

Domestic canines are faithful companions to humans, with a strong desire to serve. Their ability to love, even after suffering abuse, is incredible. I don't think all dogs love all people unconditionally, but I have seen how they have the capacity to forgive, forget and love again, even after going through very tough times. Do they ever forget their past? I don't know the answer to that, but I have certainly seen with my own eyes how a little bit of love and care can literally change everything about a dog. And that's how I decided what I wanted to do next: to be a hands-on agent of change in the lives of these neglected dogs.

PART 2

Building a Dog's Trust

The work of a canine carer volunteer

Animals are such agreeable friends –
they ask no questions, they pass no criticisms.

GEORGE ELIOT

In the work I had done with *Animal A&E,* I had never seen what happened to the dogs after the rescue. I really wanted to see the whole journey of rehabilitation, and I wanted to be in some small way part of it.

While filming the one-hour special for TV3 on why Ireland is the puppy farming capital of Europe back in 2011, I had worked closely with Dogs Trust, and I was hugely impressed by the dedication and commitment of all of the team there, from the highest level all the way down to the volunteers. I had an idea that I would like to somehow get involved personally, starting at the bottom as a canine carer volunteer.

In terms of being successful in gaining employment within Dogs Trust, it's always beneficial for canine carers to have some form of experience working with dogs, particularly in a similar environment. That said, I didn't have any formal training, while other candidates would undoubtedly have completed one of the range of courses available, which cover all areas of canine health, welfare, behaviour and training. So without any traditional, formal training in working with dogs, I needed, first and foremost, to prove to Dogs Trust that I was genuine in my passion to be responsible for the wellbeing of the dogs in my care. Dogs Trust want every member of staff to make a difference to the lives of the dogs in the centre and provide them with the best possible care they can, and I needed to show I could fit in as one of the team. I had to convince them I was there to be of service and, somewhere along the way, I had to get their permission to allow our film cameras to capture all the special moments.

In 2014 I began having meetings with Suzie Carley, Dogs Trust's PR and communications manager, about the possibility of filming a pilot for a new show in which I would train to become a canine carer volunteer with Dogs Trust. It would entail working with dogs that had, for whatever reason, found themselves in a pound, abandoned or given over to the care of the welfare organisation. When the cameras started rolling, I would be part of their journey to recovery, hopefully right up until the moment when they found their forever home.

This was the first time I had generated my own idea for a series, and it felt nerve-wracking and wonderful all at once. It was entirely my gig, so if it failed, I'd only have myself to blame. I explained to Suzie that I would shoulder the cost of filming and I described to her how I imagined the series unfolding. Thankfully, she got behind the project with passion from the very beginning. She had previously owned her own successful production company earlier in her career, so she could see the potential of my vision for the series. She kindly cleared her diary and on a cold day in September of that same year, 2014, I was allowed to bring in a small film crew for a tour and to do a recce for the project and also, hopefully, film some little snippets of the daily activities.

For me, visiting the Dogs Trust centre in Finglas, Dublin, was a real eye-opener. There was so much to take in. I knew it was Ireland's largest dog welfare charity and the centre had been specially built for purpose in November 2009, but I had no concept of just how big it was. I thought I would be focusing on the dogs in the main, long, central rehoming block. The largest block is the rehoming area, which has twenty-four kennels, and this is the corridor every member of the public sees when they visit Dogs Trust. If you have visited the centre, you will know this long corridor well, as it is behind the main reception area when you walk into the facility. It is pretty impressive in itself, as the kennels were carefully designed for the dogs' comfort and are also environmentally friendly – the building is designed to harvest all rainwater, which is then used for cleaning the kennels, and to flush the toilets at the centre, too. The dogs in the kennels enjoy under-floor heating and specially designed sniffing holes so they can 'meet' their potential new family for the first time.

However, I quickly found out that the rehoming block is just the beginning of the maze that is Dogs Trust HQ. There is so much more to this highly organised centre than most might see on first appearances. The first surprise was that the centre is built on a six-acre site, which I hadn't anticipated. They have a huge amount of space to play with, and they make every centimetre count.

On arrival you are met by the reception team, who are the front-of-house staff, dealing with the public who come to adopt a dog. The reception area is a hive of activity as it also houses a training barn and staff offices above, with a little shop below for dog treats and leads. The star attraction in this area, however, is the 'Dog of the Week'. Here, a dog who is being regularly overlooked by visitors is given a chance to shine. He or she will spend the day as 'Dog of the Week', occupying a special large glass kennel that is the focal point of the reception area. This way, the dog meets everyone who enters the reception area, in the hope that he or she will stand out and be adopted by their special someone. Each Dog of the Week gets some extra care and attention lavished on them by the staff, and an opportunity to meet everyone who walks into the centre that day. This exposure very often leads to them being booked to be adopted.

So, why would a dog get overlooked? Well, there are actually seventy-nine large kennels in total at the centre, and fifty-five are those are out of sight of the public. It's often one of these unseen dogs that is chosen to be showcased as Dog of the Week, giving them a chance to take centre-stage and make a case for themselves.

On that first day of recce with the film crew, we had to tear ourselves away from the bustle and fun of the reception area as comedian PJ Gallagher had dropped in with his dog, Lilo, who had previously been adopted from the charity. PJ was looking at the sweet Pit Bull, Spencer, who had caught his eye in the Dog of the Week kennel.

I knew I needed to focus on becoming familiar with the logistics of the facility. Once I had adjusted to its huge size, the next challenge was to map it out in my head, so that I understood the different areas and how they were interlinked. It wouldn't do to get lost in this maze! I admired the confidence and ease of movement of the staff. It was clear that everyone knew where he or she needed to be, what they needed to do and how to go about doing it. I asked Suzie how this was organised, and she described how it was sorted out in detail at the daily morning meeting.

My first question was: how will I know what to do?

Suzie explained how it worked. 'After the meeting, tasks are allocated and everything is accounted for, like the daily walk charts for each block area, where walks and training sessions are recorded, also daily dog mixes and kennel moves that are arranged and communicated on whiteboards. The team of canine carers will communicate in person and by radio to arrange all walks and mixes needed to maximise the kennel space, and often we have to help more needy dogs and arrange fun social time for the dogs in our care.'

I hadn't noticed before that, but now I saw that all the canine carers, in addition to their distinctive green uniform, carried a spare lead and a walkie talkie. These seemingly rudimentary tools were central to ongoing, effective communication needed all day, every day. I didn't quite understand at first why it was so important to have over thirty walkie-talkies about the place, but it soon become clear.

The centre is run with military precision, and it has to be that way because there can be up to 200 dogs at any one time requiring care. I suppose, like many first-time volunteers, I expected to be playing with dogs and frolicking with cute puppies all day, but the reality was very different. What you may end up doing as a volunteer can be far from what you imagined. In my mind, I knew I would need to provide food and water for all dogs in my care, exercise them, maybe administer medicine and groom them as directed, but I was to learn that there was so much more involved than that.

After giving us the initial welcome and overview, Suzie handed us over to Catriona Birt, the centre's manager, for the grand tour. Catriona is a wee dark-haired lass from Scotland who has been at the centre from its inception, transferring in from Dogs Trust UK. She led us past the familiar areas and straight into the additional adult kennelling area, which is called 'booked block'. This houses the lucky dogs who have been booked to go to their forever homes, so the dogs here are constantly changing and mixing.

Catriona then brought us into an area called 'new arrivals' and 'adult screening'. These blocks house adult dogs who have recently arrived to the centre, generally from the pound. They can require an awful lot of TLC because they can be both sick and overwhelmed by the whole experience. I met Andy and John, the canine carers assigned to this block who explained they are the first to meet the new arrivals and assess their personalities and characters. I found it quite overwhelming being in there, seeing just how many different dogs and breeds had been abandoned and rejected by their owners. It's a hard thing for an animal lover like me to understand. I felt there was a sadness about the block as these new arrivals seemed lost and quite unsure about everything.

Then we moved on to the low-stress kennels, which I didn't have much interaction with initially. They are designed to provide a tranquil and calm environment for dogs suffering from anxiety or stress. We quietly moved away from the low-stress kennels, and on to the dedicated vet suite, which is like a mini animal hospital. It is centrally located in the heart of the facility, with easy access from all locations. There was a team of four busily working away when we dropped in: the vet, the vet nurse, a dedicated vet suite canine carer and the vet administrator. It is a state-of-the-art veterinary suite, including a small animal theatre and a recovery kennel area. It also houses a separate isolation area for any dogs that need to be quarantined, should they have any contagious illness that requires barrier nursing.

Jenny, the vet nurse, explained that the canine parvovirus (CPV) is a highly contagious viral illness that affects dogs. The virus manifests itself in two different forms: intestinal and cardiac. The intestinal form is the most common form and is characterised by vomiting, diarrhea, weight loss and lack of appetite. The less common form is the cardiac form, which attacks the heart muscles of very young puppies, often leading to death.

It's a dreadful illness once it takes hold in a dog population, so monitoring new arrivals is of paramount importance. The vet team is extremely careful with any dogs showing any signs of the illness.

The thought of such a debilitating disease spreading and being potentially dangerous to all the dogs in their care really shook me. As I stood silently thinking about this, I noticed something: the noise level had completely changed. Yes, I was in silent contemplation, but there was no barking, instead there was a constant hum and buzz that was very distracting. I realised it was coming from the team's walkie-talkies, the hum of the myriad conversations being transmitted by the radios. I asked the vet nurse why everyone was on radio and she said looked at me in surprise. She admitted she didn't even notice it anymore, but that the radio contact was necessary to alert staff to any problems, and also for quick clearance of certain areas when moving dogs from A to B. Really, it was for the safety of the humans and the dogs.

For my next stop, I went to meet the youngest members of the centre – the newborns in their four dedicated puppy blocks. They are located beside the whelping unit, which was very quiet during that first visit. I could hear lullabies playing in the background, and it felt a very calm and reassuring place. There is also a screening unit here for the new mums, and they seemed a little more vocal, although nothing compared to the puppy rehoming areas. The puppy block was full of life, with healthy puppies jumping, playing, looking for cuddles, and not forgetting food! It was feeding time when we stopped by on our tour and it was actually hilarious – they are the best magicians I have ever seen, the food disappeared in seconds! But it was so noisy. Puppy block has a unique sound, the whimpers, yelps, howls and barks are very sweet, very distinctive and, together in unison, very loud. I had to raise my voice when asking questions about the day-to-day order of things as I tried to plot out how we might film the series.

We then followed two of the carers, called puppy-rearers, outside, where they put a litter of puppies into a large blue container to carry them outside to the sensory garden. It was sight to behold. I looked at the cameraman and he knew what I was thinking. He started filming it and mouthed to me: 'TV GOLD!'

Where these tiny little rascals were headed was a puppy's paradise. The sensory garden has a number of different surfaces, such as grass, concrete, wood, trees and tunnels, so

vaccinated puppies can get to experience different sensations beneath their paws before they are adopted. It was adorable to see them jumping around having fun, and it was hard to believe that the staff didn't put them in their pockets and take them all home!

After all the excitement of the puppies, we then went on a walk around the grounds to see the six exercise compound areas. Many of the compounds were in use, and we watched dogs doing agility training, having fun time with the volunteers, while others were being mixed with new dogs to see if they would make good kennel mates.

Just when I thought we must have seen everything, we were brought to the two large exercise fields. It was like being in the middle of the countryside. I couldn't believe it. The fields were long and spacious, with beautiful green grass and a profusion of beautiful flowers. It made me think of *Little House on the Prairie*! Everything was perfect, until the weather took a turn for the worse and it began to rain. I was getting ready to run for cover when I noticed no one else seemed to be that bothered. This is Ireland, after all, so the staff ignored the weather and just got on with doing whatever had to be done. The weather, just like the frequent noise of airplanes passing overhead (the centre is located close to Dublin airport), was continuously changing and accepted, so that no one noticed it anymore. I mentioned their hardiness to Catriona, and she smiled. She gently pointed out that having in excess of 150 dogs at any one time, who all needed to be exercised and socialised daily, meant the weather had to be completely ignored. It was just another part of the job.

At that point Catriona's radio crackled into life and she was called back to reception, so we made our return with her. As we walked, my crew expressed their concern about the noise levels both in and outside of the centre, and the possibility that it would interrupt filming. They described it as 'non-stop barking', much to Catriona's amusement, and wondered if there was anything that could be done about it. Once again, Catriona gently explained that most animals in any shelter are overwhelmed, and it can be a big adjustment for them to adapt to their new surroundings. She assured the team that while the dogs like to bark out their hellos, when you get to know them and they get comfortable around you, then they tend not to bark so much. I wasn't sure if my team were reassured, but I figured we'd work it out as we went along. You couldn't make a series about dogs and not expect a volley of barks from time to time.

We were nearly at reception when we passed a man on a small grass-cutter. Catriona beckoned him over and introduced us to as the lovely Mark, or Mark Maintenance as he is fondly known among the staff. I would learn that Mark was as capable as they come, tackling every manner of job, from fixing kennels to grass cutting to finding lost keys. He told Catriona he had just located a lost key, as it happened, tracking it to one of the many cars used by the staff for home visits. Catriona immediately radioed one of the training and behavioural assistants, or TBAs, to tell her to come collect the missing key, so she could get on her way to a home visit to help a recently rehomed dog settle in. Catriona told us that the dog had been a long-term resident and everyone wanted to make sure the transition went smoothly.

My impression of the centre was that it worked like a well-oiled machine, while everyone was very chatty, it was clear they were very busy, with no one ever slacking off, certainly not that we saw. We had reached reception by now, but Catriona's radio was buzzing again, and this time it was Suzie asking her to come upstairs. The upstairs office is where a team of twenty-one manage the campaigns, fundraising, PR, accounts and educational side of things. Catriona showed us up to the office, then she handed us back to Suzie while she raced off to attend to the many jobs that needed her attention. Suzie brought us up to the boardroom, which had a large glass window overlooking the rehoming corridor, and there she introduced us to the centre's Executive Director at the time, Mark Beazley.

Mark spoke to us about the charity and about how it operated. With seventy percent of the dogs in their care coming in from pounds, he wanted me to meet the dedicated ambulance driver, Ian, who carried out the weekly rescues and Ian's wife, Fiona, who headed up the educational side of the charity. I was diligently trying to keep up and write notes on every word he was saying, but then he said something that completely confused me.

'Sorry, did you just say you live on-site?', I asked.

I had noticed houses to the side of the facility, but I hadn't questioned who might live there. Smiling, Mark told us that, yes, he did live there, as did the centre's manager Cat, as she was known to her colleagues, and a few other members of the team. I was taken aback at first, but then I quickly realised it made sense given that the centre needs to operate 24/7, 365 days a year! As Mark said, 'even on

Christmas day the dogs need to be walked and cared for, it's business as usual.' The facility is always working and someone must always be there, or at least on call. Mark made a joke about taking his work home with him, but really, I admired the level of dedication of these people who lived, breathed and slept their vocation towards these dogs' welfare. I pitched my proposal and, to my delight, Mark was fully on board and so was the Dogs Trust team it seemed, but that was just the first hurdle. The small bit of filming we did during those early days became the short pilot that I pitched to TV3, and it was almost two years later that the show was commissioned by Lynda McQuaid, in 2016. Sometimes in TV you have to have patience and commitment to your vision, and I did. So finally, almost two years since that first September day in 2014, the series *Dog Tales with Andrea Hayes*, became a reality and was aired on Irish television screens for the first time.

After all that anticipation, getting the green light was a sudden jolt of reality for me as I was now an actual canine carer-in-training and I had to do the work. I was very nervous on my first day as a carer, particularly as lots had changed since the filming for the pilot: I had a larger and different crew, and Suzie's role was to change too, as she soon would become the new executive director. She and Cat would be overseeing the whole film shoot, and of course the dogs had changed too. But as I stood there, trying to calm down and get my bearings, something sounded so familiar that it put me at ease: the distinctive noise of barking, the hum of radio banter and the distant sound of low-flying aircrafts passing overhead.

From day one, from hour one, I had to quickly get used to one very constant thing in the life of a canine carer – the amount of cleaning they do! I think it is fair to say that to work with Dogs Trust, you need to like cleaning just as much as you like dogs. A typical day for the team starts at 8.00 a.m., with a brief planning meeting where everyone is assigned duties. After that, it's breakfast time, followed by the first long walk of the day. While this is going on, another team is standing by to begin the hard maintenance work – cleaning up all the 'presents' left from the night before, removing all the bedding and toys for washing and replacing them with fresh bedding, and getting the kennel fresh and clean for the new day ahead. The cleaning doesn't stop there as the dogs' dishes have to be washed, laundry has to be done, and if new dogs are due to arrive, their kennels have to be deep-cleaned as well. Every area imaginable is disinfected to maintain the highest standard of cleanliness. This isn't just for the animal accommodation either, the rigorous cleaning extends to the isolation and exercise areas, food preparation areas and surrounding outside areas, even the drains are deep cleaned every day. And all of that cleaning has to be finished by midday, when it's time to serve lunch. After lunch, the afternoon shift follows a similar pattern, with emphasis on exercise and training and maybe following up with the vets and the medical teams. There is never, ever a dull moment as there is always something to do. Every task is documented, which means detailed reports, like kennel diaries, food charts and behaviour and health assessments, are another aspect of the daily chores.

That is just some of the work going on behind-the-scenes and then there is the front-of-house work. The charity receives an average of fifty calls a day from the public, and they also have to deal with visitors who wish to view dogs with the intention of adopting one, people returning with their adopted dogs for scheduled spaying or neutering operations in their on-site vet suite, plus there are always things you can't plan for, like the unexpected arrival of stray dogs being dropped in by members of the public. They are also constantly talking to the pounds and other welfare organisations around the country, organising transportation of new dogs to the facility: when one dog goes out, the space is filled immediately by pound operations administrator Sorcha Conlon. Communication is key to everything they do – they must have great interpersonal skills and be a strong team player to ensure everything runs perfectly, safely and efficiently.

They are dealing with dogs of all shapes and sizes, and every aspect needs to be considered before they can take a dog into their care. Sometimes, though, they don't even have time to organise themselves, as dogs have been simply dumped at the facility, or even thrown over the gates in a pitiful state, so they must then shuffle all the others around to make room for them somewhere. It is fair to say that there is never an empty kennel, or an office without a dog being cared for.

The main aim for everyone is to get every dog well, fully rehabilitated and rehomed into a suitable forever home, so this is the priority. As a carer you can often be out on home visits, or involved in the busy adoption days that take place twice a week. These days are always bittersweet, and they are generally busy days at the centre as the new families meet in reception before going into the training barn for the pre-adoption talk, then family by family they are called and their dog is brought up to them, the old collar is removed and a new one is put on, and before the lead is passed over, they double check the microchip is accurate and correct. Often there can be many canine carers waving off some of the longer term residents.

In addition to all that is the often unseen work taking place upstairs in the office, such as lobbying the government for change on animal welfare issues, like online selling of animals, the Dog Breeding Establishment Act and the Welfare of Greyhounds Act, as well as creating a dog-friendly society and much more. The charity is also committed to ongoing education about responsible dog ownership and Fiona and her team work nationwide educating all ages about how to 'Be Dog Smart'.

Everyone, from senior management to volunteers, has a part to play and everyone has an important role. Like any job, some days are great, some days are sad, and others are just hard. During my time as a volunteer I went through a whole blend of emotions, there were many tears of joy, but also some tinged with sadness. You come to know and love the animals, so it can be hard to see them leave the centre. Of course, you are thrilled for them and that's what it is all about, but it is so easy to get attached to the animals and to miss them once they have been adopted. Sometimes you find yourself wondering and worrying about how they are settling into their new home. I tell myself that they have gone to a carefully chosen, loving home that has been assessed by the Dogs Trust staff, and that's all that matters.

Other days I found myself crying for a dog that was still resident in the centre. It is absolutely heartbreaking to see a super animal get overlooked when so many who have come in after them seem to get rehomed. You anxiously think to yourself: what more can I do to give them the best chance of adoption? I end up playing out scenarios in my head of how I could buy a bigger property and save them all, but it's simply not feasible.

You have to grow thick skin in this job and learn to separate your emotions from what you need to do. Sometimes seeing the physical neglect a dog may have suffered can overwhelm you, but you have to put your own feelings on hold and focus on the dog and what he or she needs. Sometimes you will see animals in pain, dealing with injuries, trying to recover from abuse, or even being returned after being adopted (we call these dogs RTK – returned to kennel). These are normal animal rescue occurrences that do happen and are part of the day-to-day, but so are kennel cuddles and plenty of free runs and fun with the dogs in your care.

It wasn't easy, in fact I found the work of a canine carer very challenging, but when I left each day I knew I was part of something very special and magical. I learned so much about life, love and the human condition by being among the dogs and their carers. There is nothing more gratifying to me than developing a bond with an animal, seeing the trust grow between us, and then the effect of that relationship – how they can get back on their paws again and thrive. Being part of that process has been life-altering.

Working with rescue dogs has been a cathartic, healing experience for me. I can tell you that volunteering at a charity like Dogs Trust is so rewarding, and the overall experience totally changed me as a person. It isn't all kennel cuddles, it is very hard work, but it's also fulfilling, fun, humbling and deeply satisfying. Like all charities, Dogs Trust needs support, so if you can give your time and support, I would recommend it highly. You can help to ensure they can continue their endless care of animals.

It sounds like a cliché, but working as a canine carer can be a roller-coaster of emotions in just one day, and then you have to do it all again the next day. But it is worth it to see so many wagging tails, and to leave each evening knowing these rescued dogs will get a second chance at happiness. The happiness that they give back to you in return is hard to put into words. I have seen how these animals have brought joy and love into their new home, and I often wonder: who really saved whom?

Maybe these animals are angels in disguise. It often seems like the right owner and that special dog come into each other's lives at the perfect time for a miracle to occur. Each provides joy, healing, patience, courage, gratitude and, of course, unconditional love – the perfect virtues often missing in society.

I am so grateful for my time as a canine carer. Under the roof of the Dogs Trust facility, all life is played out, and the dogs' life stories can teach us much. So I'd like to share the stories of some of the four-legged friends I made during my time as a carer.

These are their Dog Tales.

Name:	Penny
Breed:	Pit Bull crossbreed

Arrived to Dogs Trust:

Penny arrived to Dogs Trust from another rescue organisation. She was heavily pregnant.

Dogs Trust History:

Penny gave birth to eleven puppies the day after arriving at Dogs Trust, but sadly six of them passed away. Penny was a great mum and looked after her puppies really well.

When she moved out of the puppy block, Penny was found to be confident and very social with other dogs.

She is an amazingly friendly girl and was an immediate favourite of every carer who came into contact with her.

Type of Home Required:

Children aged 10+

Penny is a total love bug and will make a great addition to anybody's home. She loves people and is very friendly.

PENNY
The joys of puppy love

Dogs, for a reason that can only be described as divine, have the ability to forgive, let go of the past, and live each day joyously. It's something the rest of us strive for.

JENNIFER SKIFF

On my first day, and my first official meeting with all my fellow staff took place at 8.00 a.m. Cat introduced me formally to the staff, and they were told that Suzie would answer any questions they had about the film crew that would be shadowing me. Cat made it very clear to everyone I was going to get 'stuck in'. She handed me my official badge and uniform, and suddenly there was no turning back. This was it. I was a canine carer and I'd have to prove myself quickly.

After a quick change, I was ready. I felt different walking around in the distinctive green aertex top, green fleece and black trousers, with my official badge. As soon as I began moving around the centre, I was often stopped by members of the public and asked about a dog, or asked where to leave blankets they were dropping off. They didn't know I was a nervous newbie. I was now part of the team and, to be honest, even the dogs reacted differently, and didn't bark as much because the uniform was so familiar to them.

That first day was a gentle introduction – meeting the other carers, getting to know the ropes, meeting the dogs, getting another overview of the facility and still trying to remember all the routes and rooms. It was an easy day, and I was ready for a bigger challenge.

The next day I started work as a volunteer. In the morning meeting, I was assigned to the maternity unit. I made my way there after the meeting, delighted that this was my first assignment. It seemed like the perfect place to start – the idea of being the one to welcome new life into the world and nurture these newborn puppies and help mum at this critical time in her life was heartwarming. Little did I know I would face some big challenges, both physically and emotionally.

My day started with some instructions from Cat as we walked down to the whelping bays. Cat explained the history of the state-of-the-art puppy accommodation unit, that it was a much-needed extension to the Rehoming Centre, and that she knew it had already saved hundreds of additional puppies. As someone who had seen first-hand the unspoken and often unseen reality and fallout of surging levels of puppies being abandoned across the country, I felt really thrilled to be able to make a difference.

When we reached the unit, I was immediately struck by how calm and quiet it was, which stood in sharp contrast to the noise levels in other areas of the centre. Here, what first struck me were the peaceful, hushed sounds that greeted me when I walked inside. It brought me right back to when I was nursing my daughter, Brooke, as there was a familiar lullaby CD playing in the background. I also noticed the curtains pulled across the middle of the floor, so the dogs weren't eyeballing each other on opposite sides. I could see that everything was being done to ensure the comfort of the expectant mums. The staff had created a Zen environment, just right for a labour ward. The canine mums were obviously the priority, which ensured that their newborns would have a healthy and safe start in life.

After the initial overview, it was time to get a full run-down from Cat on each dog I would be caring for that day. There was a variety of dogs and puppies, each needing different care. Some had already had their puppies; some needed a little extra help with feeding; while others were waiting patiently to whelp. Cat gives me and the other carers assigned to the maternity unit all the information we needed, and we quickly split the workload between us. As the newest, most enthusiastic member of the team, I was keen to get started, but I was tasked with observing and learning first, to see and understand what the team did every day.

Not surprisingly, there was lots to be done, and the group spread out and quietly got on with the work. They had to monitor the new arrivals, which is challenging when there can be anything up to eight puppies in a litter. They told me they had recently had a litter of fourteen! It was not just the newborns who needed vigilant monitoring, some of the pregnant mums were almost ready to whelp, so everyone had to keep a close eye on them! To be honest, I wasn't sure what we were looking for, so I was happy to observe the team as they explained that they were monitoring temperature changes, nesting behaviour and even refusal to eat food. Any such behaviour can indicate that birth is imminent, so everything was documented and tracked.

We had to clean the bedding, which meant disposing of their little leavings – and sometimes not so little! Then we moved on to feeding. Luckily, there was a feeding board to make things easier, listing the different mixes for every dog. Each dog is unique, so their mixes were drawn up depending on what they need. Some of the pups needed to be supported with bottle feeding, and that took up a lot of time and was repeated every two hours.

So far I had helped out at being cleaner and chef, now it was time to learn how to be a nurse in order to administer medication to those who needed it. It really was non-stop. No moment was wasted, and these puppy-rearers worked diligently and with complete focus. I watched as they performed miraculous feats of juggling as more mums and puppies arrived, requiring other pups to be moved on to a different part of the facility. I had only observed and helped around the edges, but it was still a demanding and exhausting shift. I had huge admiration for the staff, I can tell you.

So, day two – time to step up and take on a full role as a carer. Cat greeted me when I arrived that morning, smiling widely and telling me I was going to love it. We chatted about her time at the centre, and she told me that since opening in 2009, the charity had rehomed almost 13,000 dogs. Cat had been there from the start, which meant she had been part of every dog's story. As she said to me, 'If I had a penny for every dog that has changed my life, I would be a very rich woman!' We went into the morning meeting to receive our assignments, and it turned out that Penny was the name of the very first dog I was going to care for and be responsible for. It felt like a good omen!

Cat once again walked me to the maternity unit, where she introduced me to fantastic new mum Penny and told me this brave dog's incredible story.

Penny had arrived from an animal sanctuary that couldn't care for her in the situation they found her in. It was immediately obvious, by the sheer size of her abdomen, that she was heavily pregnant and the sanctuary looked to Dogs Trust to help this unwanted Pit Bull mum-to-be. She had only spent one night in the whelping unit before giving birth. Astonishingly, she had a litter of eleven beautiful puppies early the next morning. Sadly, not all of the litter survived, but for new mum Penny and her five little ones, their journey of care began at the centre.

The young puppies totally depended on their mother for the first few weeks, and she was a loving and attentive mum. After about two weeks the little puppies opened their eyes, and they stole the hearts of everyone they met. These five little puppies hadn't lost their cuteness when I met them a few weeks later.

Penny was a very beautiful and kind new mum. She was larger than life and seemed well able to manage her lively litter of Pit Bull crossbreed puppies. They were full of personality and energy and my first job was to try to learn all their names, which had been inspired by pigs, of all things! Canine carer Sarah helped me adjust to my new friends, and really my first few days with them involved simply sitting with them, playing with them, teaching them their names and giving them a little bit of praise if they acknowledged it. This was a great opportunity for me to get to know them, and also to give exhausted mum Penny a little break. The kennels are designed in such a way to separate the puppies and mum with a small barrier, just enough for mum to step over for a break, but so she can still keep a watchful eye over her fast-growing brood.

During my daily visits with the pups I learned that every playful interaction had a purpose. I was trying to teach these little guys focus and attention, and good personal skills with humans. This sounds easy, but trust me, just like little toddlers' attention spans are short, so are puppies'. But as my first few days flew past, I was learning more every day and my confidence as a canine carer was growing. Each day we all did a little better, and every single time a puppy looked at me when I called their name, or even if I could gain their focus, I would say a proud, 'Yes!' and treat them secretly. I was saying 'yes' to myself, too. I was so happy that I was actually bedding into the role.

I learned so much about a puppy's formative first weeks during my first week in the maternity unit. While mum is vitally important, we have a role with these little ones too. Building a healthy bond with the puppies was so rewarding, and who doesn't like cuddling a puppy? But not too much, as I was told many times by my supervisor. We also had to allow them to run around and interact and find their own feet. It was fascinating to watch how Penny would show them love when they had earned it. I could see how puppies need that leader role.

Over time they learned to respect and trust me. More importantly, each day that passed, my admiration for Penny was growing. She was a selfless mum, never complaining despite five hungry, strong, growing Pit Bull puppies all vying for attention and food!

My first week was soon over – the days go very fast when you're so busy. I headed into week two feeling buoyed by all the tiny little victories of week one and a new sense of confidence. That week, the puppies were getting ready to wean from mum and the process of separation began. They slowly began to transition from nursing to eating solid food, which opened a new chapter for them and their amazing mum.

The puppies were almost ready for the rehoming unit and, hopefully, adoption, but before they could be unleashed on the public, I was given the important task of bathing this lively litter. It was my first time to do it, and I wasn't sure who would be more anxious, me or them. I told myself to breathe: 'If you're stressed, the puppies will pick up on your emotions and they will become anxious. Stay calm, Andrea!'

Despite my best efforts, the excitable little ones just saw this as more playtime. They dashed around the plastic container, sniffing it out, they soon began rolling on the lovely soft towels I had placed out next to it. One pup held back, not as confident or sure as his siblings. I eyed him, fearing trouble. But I had to face my fears, it was time to pick up the first one and introduce him to the water.

My heart was pounding. I remembered bathing my baby daughter for the first time and I had that same nervous feeling that I might do something wrong.

I got the first puppy in and out safely, placing him on a comfy warm bed. I was starting to get into my stride. I found a little shampoo goes a long way, and I was starting to sort of enjoy it. Just as I felt I was getting the hang of it, it was time for the little nervous guy. I had left him until the end. He didn't like the water at all, and immediately made a bid for freedom and tried to jump back out. Just as he was doing that, one of the more confident siblings was trying to get back in! I managed to swoop him up in one hand and wrap him back up in a towel, as I gently rinsed off the one in the tub with the other hand. Luckily, one of team offered to lend a hand and order was restored, and soon all the puppies were washed, dry, warm, sleeping and ready to go to their new kennels. We brought them to the rehoming unit and handed them over to their new carers.

Back at the maternity unit, I wondered what it was like for Penny, not having her little ones around. We had all got so used to their little noises and behaviours, they were a very active bunch, so I really felt their absence. When I spoke to some of the other carers, they seemed to miss them too. Everyone gets attached, but separation is part of the job and you have to get used to it. I wondered if we'd be separated from Penny very soon too, but as I was soon to learn, lots more rehabilitation work had to happen for Penny.

Her little puppies slowly become a much quieter pack in their new kennel and it didn't take long for them to be booked for adoption. One by one they left to start their lives in new, loving homes. Only one little puppy remained, called Porkie (who sadly is still at the centre to this day, which breaks my heart)

I asked if I could continue to be part of Penny's journey. The team made it a priority to get her into the right home. We had some work to do first, though, because, given her breed, she would have to be muzzled in public. Under the Control of Dogs Act, certain dogs are required by law to wear a muzzle in a public place. This was going to be the first time I had trained any dog to wear a muzzle, so I was nervous – again! I wasn't at all afraid of Penny, so it wasn't because of fear, I just didn't know what to do, and I am sure she didn't know what a muzzle was. But as ever I had the brilliant team of trainers around to help me – and Penny – undertake this brand new challenge.

Prior to working with Dogs Trust, whenever I had seen a muzzle on a dog, I always believed it was because the animal was aggressive, but that is so wrong. There is an association made between danger and muzzles, and while they are not the most attractive and do tend to make a dog look a bit like Hannibal Lector, in truth they are used for safety.

To my surprise, I realised that pretty much every dog was muzzle-trained, from the big to the very small. They all get used to wearing a muzzle while at the centre. The reasoning behind this makes sense: for any new owner, they know the dog is used to having a muzzle, which can be very helpful when they are visiting the vet or socialising with other dogs and, of course, it prevents biting.

So how do you teach an adult dog to like muzzles? You make it fun, and messy. I discovered Penny loved peanut butter, so this was my treat of choice when trying to persuade her to put it on. I got into a routine of bringing her to one of the sensory gardens outside, where she could run around, and then I'd call her and ask her to put her mouth into the muzzle, with some peanut butter on top. She would sniff it out, put her nose in, lick it, and that was that for the first

day. I wasn't trying to close it or force it on, it was just her getting used to the touch and me getting used to doing it. I had trainer Cheryl teaching me as I was doing this training with Penny, and as if that wasn't enough pressure, Penny and I were doing all of this in front of our film crew. However, just like me, I think Penny soon forgot that the cameras were rolling and concentrated on the training.

The weather was warm and it was great to be outside, enjoying the sunshine and seeing Penny having fun. She was healing physically, too. I had spent so many days in the maternity wing, watching her feed, and this felt like a nice reward for all her hard work. Working on muzzle training brought us closer together. Lots of working together and touching and praise creates a bond, and it also produces a wonderful association between human hands and treats. Penny loved getting spoilt!

This gorgeous dog was a quick learner. She had great focus and the sticky taste of peanut butter was a big motivation, and it worked.

We took our time, and went through a lot of peanut butter, but soon the muzzle was a pleasurable experience. She liked it because it meant she got a treat, and using language like 'Yes, Penny' when she put her nose right into the muzzle soon progressed to her allowing me to fasten it. It reinforced a positive association for her, and because I had the treats, she and I became firm friends.

Within just a few days I could easily get the muzzle on and off her with ease. Full marks all around! My teacher was happy with me, and I was delighted with my progress too; Penny was a star pupil.

She still seemed a little unsure or nervous at times, and I wondered what more we could do to help her grow in confidence. It became clear that the best thing we could do now was to find her a new home, where she could truly relax. She continued to do really well on all her training assessments and quickly demonstrated that she was good with people and other animals alike. After a long road, she was finally ready to go to the rehoming corridor.

I kept a close eye on Penny, and was delighted to see that because she had impressed so many of the team, they were quick to suggest her to potential adopters. It didn't take too long before I saw a booked sign on her chart. I couldn't have been happier.

I was so invested in this lovely dog, I really wanted to be ensure everything would go to plan for her, so I asked if I could go on the home visit for Penny, to assess if the prospective new owners were suitable. I had a quiet little word with her on the way there, assuring her that I would check out her new home and report back. I felt she gave me a knowing look, as if to say, 'Tell them how wonderful I am'. That is exactly what I did.

Everything with Penny was a first for me, and now this was to be my first home visit. John, one of the longest serving members of staff, accompanied me, and we made our way to Dublin city centre to meet the prospective adopter and evaluate if his house would be suitable for

Penny. As John explained, our job was to get a 'dog's eye' view of the home and to answer any questions the owners might have as well. While people might question if a home visit is necessary, for Dogs Trust, they need to be sure that every dog is going to the right home, in order to avoid any dog being returned to the kennels; RTK is very hard on the dogs.

Penny's new owners were called Richard and Des, and it was Des who met us and showed us around the house. I watched as John did the various checks, and he was more than happy that this would be a great home for Penny.

I asked Des what had attracted them to Penny and he said, 'Sometimes you don't get what you are looking for.' They had been looking for a smaller dog, and had no intention of getting a dog as big as Penny. He told me: 'In a way, Dogs Trust chose her for us, and we totally trusted their judgement.' So it wasn't quite a love at first sight story, but when they'd heard about Penny and her loving nature, they'd felt sure they could offer her a good home.

It turned out they had big plans for Penny, as they wanted to bring her to work. Des asked us if she was good around people. I was like a proud mum telling them just how special and kind she was. 'She loves everyone and everyone loves her,' I reassured him. I told Des that I had muzzle-trained her myself, and as I waited and watched for his reaction, I was hoping he wouldn't be too put off by the requirement for Penny to wear a muzzle. He wasn't. In fact, nothing seemed too much trouble for Des and Richard. They even agreed to meet with Penny at the centre a few more times before she came home, and also agreed to join in the muzzle training of her there. They had already committed to her and wanted to do whatever was necessary to help her fit into their family. In a home of two adults, it was a perfect fit for this brave mum who was getting back on her paws.

For the next month Des and Richard regularly came out to the centre, and they took over from me and continued the training with Penny. She is a dog who likes to say hello with a big bark, and I missed her familiar call when she left to go to her new home! But I was happy to hear that, after a little uncertainty to begin with, she took to her new life and was a very busy lady. Penny now works a nine-to-five day with her owners, who have a busy practice in town. Every day she can be spotted walking the thirty-minute journey to work though the city. This city dog is a regular around town, and was even honoured in *The Humans of Dublin*, a book recording the people, and animals, of the city. Des said they are often told how striking she is, with her distinctive white marking down her nose, and that everyone at the office adores her. It seems she loves the office environment, too, and can be seen in meetings regularly. I inquired about her loud bark and it can still be heard when new people come into the office, but people get used to it, they know it's just Penny saying hello.

At the weekends, Penny likes to be by the sea – just like her little puppies, she loves the water. For holidays, she

enjoys going to see Richard's extended family in Laois. It seemed Penny had a busier lifestyle than most, and I was absolutely thrilled for this amazing dog. Des explained how she is always with them, in work, at home and at weekends – it doesn't matter where they are going, she goes with them, and can be seen sitting outside cafes in the capital enjoying a doggy-cappuccino. She has found confidence in her new pack.

They say home is where the heart is, and that seems to be true for Penny. Like every true romance, there is plenty of laughter too for this household. Des speaks of her lovingly, and it's clear they are besotted with one another.

'Since she arrived she makes us laugh and smile every day. It's incredible how much love can fit into a dog. We love her, and I can't even imagine life without her.'

When I go home and see my Dash, I know exactly what Des means. A house with a dog is a happier place – it's a proper home.

Name:	Alex
Breed:	Jack Russell

Arrived to Dogs Trust:

Alex was tied to a road sign and abandoned outside the Dogs Trust centre.

Dogs Trust History:

Alex was found to be a friendly, happy little dog.
He was initially nervous having his harness put on.
He loved to be out and about, sniffing out his latest adventure.

Alex got on well with other dogs at the centre, and even walked by other barking dogs without reacting.

He was particularly fond of tennis balls, although he was reluctant to give them back!

Type of Home Required:

Children aged 10+

A family committed to giving Alex mental and physical exercise. Alex will make a great addition to a lucky family.

ALEX
Abandoned, but all is not lost

Saving one dog will not change the world, but surely for that one dog, the world will change forever.

KAREN DAVISON

When I was a child, one of my closest companions and dearest friends was a neighbour's dog called Judy. She was a soft old girl who allowed me to spend hours playing and chatting with her. She tagged along as I solved mysteries and chased butterflies, and every day I looked forward to seeing her. She was loyal and dutiful; she seemed to be waiting for me when I finished school.

It was a different time then, when dogs could wander freely around the neighbourhood. I grew up in the 1980s, and no one fenced in or leashed their dogs in on our road. Often, Judy would just show up at the door and sit outside until I came out.

I have vivid memories of sitting in the front garden in the summer sun, grooming her beautiful hair. Despite my constant tugging and rubbing, she was gentle and kind, in fact, she seemed to be patience personified. Although she wasn't our dog, we treated her like one of the family. I remember being so upset when she stopped calling, but she was old now and preferred to stay put in her own house. For the short time I had her as a friend, she showed me how strong the bond could be between a dog and a young child. To this day, I think of her often, and it was the essence of Judy's unconditional love, patience and sweet nature that came to mind when I first met Alex.

Sadly, his story doesn't start very well. Alex came into the care of Dogs Trust in very shocking circumstances. We don't know much about his past, and we don't know why he found himself in the unthinkable place that he did, but he was abandoned. CCTV footage captured the dreadful situation unfolding right outside the centre, which is located on a very dangerous road next to the busy Roadstone quarry. After Alex was found, the staff checked the camera, and sure enough, it had recorded it all.

It was a Saturday morning at 10.30 a.m., a very busy time for trucks and lorries heading to and from the quarry. On the screen, a lone man is seen slowing down his car and pulling up outside the front gate of the centre. The man gets out of his car and walks with the dog for a short distance. What happened next really upset me, and seeing it captured on camera was very chilling. The man loosely ties the defenceless dog to a pole and then walks away without a backward glance. He gets into the car and drives off, leaving a bewildered and distressed dog barking forlornly after him.

Watching the dog jumping in the air, desperately barking after the man, was heartbreaking. But it was his persistent barks and cries that alerted a staff member that a dog was distressed. Not knowing where the cries were coming from, but knowing it was close by, the search began. It wasn't long before he was rescued from outside the facility and brought into safety.

When I watched the footage afterwards, I was pretty angry. It was tough to watch, and hard to believe the owner just dumped this little Jack Russell next to a busy road. I couldn't understand his actions, but I can only guess there must have been a compelling reason for the man to feel he had no other option but to abandon the Jack Russell. Sadly, the charity sees this all too often. The truth is that people's situations can change, and it can be a very sad, and sometimes traumatic, situation for somebody when they can no longer look after their pet. I could never desert a dog, but the fact that he was left where he was makes me think that the owner wanted him to get a good home. We don't know other people's circumstances, so it's not fair to judge.

Before I met the little dog, I watched this footage with a member of staff, who explained to me what had happened next for this little dog. Like many animals that are abandoned, he wasn't microchipped. The team tried to get a clear view of the car's registration number, but they were unable to identify the car or the driver. The terrier was now under the care of the charity, and they gave him the new name of Alex.

When the vet team checked little Alex, he was in reasonably good health, so it was clear he was a cared-for family pet at some stage in his life. Not surprisingly, Alex was very confused and a little bit scared of his new surroundings.

I was still pretty new to these surroundings myself, so I could really empathise with Alex. We slowly built up a bond. He had a very gentle, friendly nature and after seeing the video footage, I had a bit of a soft spot for him. I told myself every day, 'We have to get Alex into a new home.' I made an effort to have some really good quality time with this special little dog as often as possible. So after a busy day on overdrive – juggling canine logistics, walking dogs, feeding, completing errands, squeezing in cleaning to-dos, finding and replacing doggy toys, meeting and greeting the public and making sure I was on top of my preparation for filming the following day – the end of my day meant time with Alex before I said goodnight.

All day, I would eagerly anticipate finding just ten minutes to chill out with him. Sometimes I would simply sit and have time with him in his kennel. That social interaction is so important for dogs in the centre, and it became just as important for me too. Alex loved to play with his tennis balls, so I would play fetch with him and just relax with him. There was something about Alex, a special energy that was very relaxing.

He didn't really like anyone touching him or rubbing him too much, and I wondered what his original name was and who might have cared for him. He was relatively young and clearly he had been house-trained, so trying to piece together the clues to make his story complete was so difficult: what could have happened? Why did this lovely dog end up here?

While I sat there, pondering his past, I would start to decompress and the stresses of the day would disappear. I began to notice over time that he had this really calming effect on me. He wasn't a lap dog and it wasn't that I was rubbing him constantly, although after a time he did trust me enough to give him lots of belly rubs, but there was something else about him. I wasn't the only one to notice it. Alex was a popular boy, with his calm nature and love of people and other dogs, he had many friends.

John was one of his carers and I trained with him to see what type of behavioural training he was doing on a daily and weekly basis with Alex. Most dog trainers use high-value food like hotdog or peanut butter when they are training, but sometimes food doesn't work. Alex turned out to be a dog who wasn't food-motivated, so non-food positive reinforcers were needed. I was surprised when John explained that Alex wasn't massively motivated by food or enrichment, because he was the first dog I'd met who was like that. Penny would have sold her soul for a bit of peanut butter! But with Alex, John figured out that he loved to please and was eager to make his handler, and others he trusted, happy. In John's opinion, this made Alex very trainable and very intelligent. He also felt that past anxiety about food could be stopping him from responding to it as well.

One thing was for sure – toys, and particularly his many balls, motivated Alex, so they were the means John used to train him. John always brought him into a low stress environment, in the training barn or maybe one of the sensory gardens, so he could really focus on work. John's commitment and hard work paid off as Alex was absolutely transformed, with lots of tricks up his fur to impress potential adopters.

Alex was the perfect companion animal, so all we needed to do was to find him the perfect human partner. After being fully assessed by the behaviour team, Alex was ready to move to the rehoming corridor, ready to catch the eye of a potential new family. I was very hopeful for him as I was really attached to the little guy, and I was sure everyone would see how he was, but the process took a little longer than I had expected. As each day ended, I was so surprised this charming dog was once again overlooked.

This was something I would have to get used to during my time at the centre. Although on paper Alex was perfect – he was good with animals, children, excellent on the lead, fully house-trained, fit, healthy and not to mention handsome – no one seemed to be interested him. I was puzzled.

I wondered if it had something to do with Alex himself – was he afraid he would be rejected again? Maybe Alex hadn't read any of the signs that things weren't working out with his previous family. He was well cared for, so I am sure he had food, human interaction and maybe even a lot of love. To Alex, things might have seemed like they were going well, and then suddenly to be abandoned by the one you love and left barking for your life, to find yourself in a strange environment with so much noise, perhaps wondering over and over again: what did I do wrong? I began to wonder if Alex could ever fully trust a human again.

I started to really look at his behaviour when visitors were wandering up and down the rehoming wing. I noticed he didn't really make eye contact. He wasn't shy, but he was more reserved and instead of jumping up like many other dogs, he would calmly hang back. I knew he needed to get into a loving home, and I made it my mission to tell every suitable potential adoptee about him. In essence, it was this slightly quieter part of his personality that most people didn't quite get, but I kept hoping that he would find his someone special.

I had been off for the weekend and when I arrived to work on Monday, I was told that Alex was booked! When an animal is booked, it means they have started the process of being adopted and the wheels of change are in motion. I was so thrilled. Before any dog leaves the centre there is the paperwork and a home visit to be completed, so I hurried to check up on that. I found out that John was booked to go to the new owner's house that afternoon, and I was keen to catch up with him on his return and find out if Alex really had found a home to call his own.

As is often the case, John reported back that the family was perfect and the home was a good match for Alex, so they would be back to collect him on adoption day in a few days' time. I was over the moon for little Alex, because I knew he truly deserved this second chance at happiness. I went down to him for some kennel cuddles, and I was welcomed with a wagging tail and a tennis ball dropped at my foot. He was excited to see me, as if he knew our time together was precious and shortly to end, and he wanted to make the most of it.

The night before adoption day, I should have been jumping for joy, but I have to admit I was really sad, knowing I wouldn't see Alex again. I wanted to make sure it was myself or John who brought him to his new family. As it happened, it was both of us. It was a soppy goodbye, we both cried, tears of joy and a little sadness. I suppose just knowing his journey to that point, I was hoping no one would break his heart or his trust again.

Nobody had prepared me for the emotions I would feel saying goodbye to the first of many doggies who would paw their way into my heart. Yes, I cried and felt a mix of emotion, but then an unexpected feeling began to overwhelm me. I felt a great sense of gratitude to Alex, that he was willing to trust me and had allowed me to become his friend in recent weeks.

The time came to hand over this kind and affectionate dog into the care to a new family. I had a chance to chat with them before we left. It seemed it was the youngest member of the family who had made the decision that Alex was for them.

The McCallum family had relocated from South Africa some years back, and after many years of searching they had recently moved into a new house. It was perfect in every way, but for this family something was missing: a family dog.

Mark was the youngest of three boys and it seems it was he who convinced the family that the time was right for the newest four-legged member to join them. Dad, Hugh, had many pet pals growing up in South Africa, so he too felt it was a great idea, but they needed to get the right dog. After much discussion, it was agreed they would all choose a dog, as a family. Some of the boys wanted big, some were looking for a smaller dog, so it wasn't going to be an easy decision to keep everyone happy. They could agree on one thing though, it should be a rescue dog. They had previously had another rescue, and they all felt they wanted to rehome a dog that needed a second chance.

They say all it takes is one day, one hour, even just one moment, a glance, and it can change your life. And that's all it took – one look.

They visited the centre as a family one Saturday, and unlike so many who had passed little Alex by, Mark explained to me that he just knew instantly this was the dog for him. They both looked at each other, and bonded, it seemed to be a kinship at first sight. They connected in that moment, and the search was over before it had barely begun. No one else had a choice in the matter. The dog was chosen, and it was Alex.

I learned a very important lesson from Alex. Everyone at Dogs Trust is part of every dog's journey to recovery and it is not about losing a dog when they leave, but about that dog gaining a permanent, loving family, a safe place they can call home. As one dog goes to his or her forever home, it makes room for another rescue journey to begin. And the story continues.

Like many of the new adopters, this family stayed in touch and sent us pictures and lovely updates on Alex. They even went so far as to invite me to drop in for a play date and a catch up with the family, which I did a few weeks later, and that's when the real transformation in Alex's story began to emerge. Out of the safe cocoon of Dogs Trust, Alex seemed to really blossom, and just like a butterfly – he was flying!

I will always remember pulling up at the family home on the day of our play date and seeing a familiar face waiting to greet me – in fact, he was sitting in the window when I rang the doorbell. I could tell he was dutifully awaiting a special arrival, but it wasn't me. Since settling in with the family, Alex's bond with all the boys had strengthened and he waited for them to return home each day from school.

As we waited for the boys, I noticed a lovely kitchen magnet that read: Jack Russells don't have owners, they have servants. It made me laugh, and I had a chat about it and it seemed Alex was the king of the castle.

After the TV show went out, he became a mini celebrity dog and all the neighbours began to know him. An artist friend of the family was so inspired by his dog tale, he took it upon himself to paint him and present the stunning portrait to the family.

What surprised me most, though, was not how great his bond was with the boys, and particularly with Mark, but how much he connected with everyone in the family and beyond! It was lovely to hear that the whole family felt more part of the local community after Alex came along. As Hugh told me, 'People stop to chat to me or my wife when we walk him locally.' A benefit from dog ownership they hadn't even considered, not only has Alex fit into the family, he has helped them fit into their new area.

Another benefit is Alex's sense of time. Apparently, he knows the routines of the house and they told me they no longer need an alarm clock as Alex is the first awake in the morning and makes sure the household never sleeps it out. Similarly, he will be waiting with his blanket at bedtime, at the same time every night. He knows when it is time for dinner, even walk time and play times are scheduled in, he seems to drop the ball just at the right time. When he isn't at the school gate waiting for Mark to come out from class, he is at the window of their new house ready to greet him on arrival. For the parents, they wanted their boys to settle into their new house and locality, and now they can't imagine life without little Alex.

I wanted to hear what the boys had to say. We had a cup of tea and chatted about Alex, and soon he started barking at the window and signaling. The wait was over!

Immediately I heard, 'Alex! Hello, boy!' Then the fun and games began.

Mark was eager to show me every new trick clever little Alex had learned, and it was impressive to see how he had responded to some consistent love, care and attention. He was jumping high, catching balls in his mouth, retrieving balls, playing hide-and-seek in the back garden and just really enjoying himself and having the time of his life. The family had immediately identified how clever this little guy was and quickly signed him up to training classes! As expected, recall was a tricky lesson to learn, which is understandable given that he was probably called something else for many years. Over time he began to respond to them and they discovered, just like we had, that he wasn't motivated by food. But they had found the perfect high-value item to get

Alex to focus – toys! And, more specifically, squeaky ones. 'He adores them,' Mark happily told me. 'He is one of the boys in our family now, and he absolutely loves playing around, sniffing out adventure and being silly.'

The rain started to fall and all the boys and little Alex came in to relax. Mark got his blanket and sat on the floor next to Alex. Gone was the dog who would shied away from cuddles and affection. As Mark rubbed his belly and played with him he told me, 'This is my favourite part of the day – coming home from school and endlessly playing ball with Alex.'

Since Alex arrived into Mark's life, they have been inseparable. Alex has grown in confidence and joy, and Mark told me he never feels lonely anymore and he knows Alex is his friend for life. 'Alex loves to be my little shadow,' Mark said, grinning at me. 'Wherever I am, you can be sure that he is not far behind. When I am sitting on the sofa, he likes to lay on the back of it and put his paws on my shoulders. He will also poke me with his nose to let me know he wants to play ball.'

Alex was staring at Mark as he spoke, and if I have ever seen a dog smiling, it was in that moment. His expression just radiated happiness and love.

I sat back in my chair and just smiled, my heart was full of joy. I felt I was, in a small way, part of this journey and I thought that maybe my prayers for this special little dog were heard and answered. He had given me so much peace and joy when I was in his company, providing a safe space for me to relax after my busy day. So to see Alex find that safety and peace in the arms of an adoring little boy was delightful.

The companionship between children and animals is well documented, but somehow the bond Alex shared with the little boy who fell in love with him at first glance was very sweet. In Mark's mind, Alex was perfect, he didn't see whatever imperfections the previous owner had seen. To Mark, Alex is his best friend. It reminded me of my younger self. Like Mark, I too was the youngest of four and like him, I loved my four-legged pal Judy, despite her imperfections.

I know Alex will forever have a special place in the hearts of his whole family and even the community, but especially in Mark's heart. He will never be forgotten, discarded or abandoned ever again. Alex is finally home.

Name:	Bumpy
Breed:	Pointer and Pitbull crossbreed

Arrived to Dogs Trust :

Bumpy arrived from Offaly pound with his littermates. They were about thirteen weeks old when they came into the care of Dogs Trust.

Dogs Trust History:

The staff had serious concerns about the health of the puppies; one of his littermates tested positive for parvovirus and had to be put into isolation. Over the first few weeks the others were closely monitored and they were all found to be thriving, except one.

Bumpy earned himself that nickname due to the accumulation of serosanguinous fluid around his occipital protuberance, at the top of his head, which had to be drained a couple of times during the first few weeks in Dogs Trust.

Type of Home Required:

A young, active family.

He is a clever, active and playful chap. He would benefit from some training on cues and self-control.

He is good around dogs and humans alike.

DogsTrust

BUMPY
Beauty is in the eye of the beholder

The great pleasure of a dog is that you make a fool of your-self with him and not only will he not scold you, he will make a fool of himself too.

SAMUEL BUTLER

A doption day at the centre is one of the busiest days of the week and also my favourite. On adoption day, all the dogs who have been booked, and whose paperwork and home visits have been completed, are collected by their new owners. So it's a hectic and emotional day for everyone, but it's also the moment when we know we've done our jobs properly, so it's a sweet moment.

I must admit, when I started working with Dogs Trust, I couldn't believe just how long and laboured the adoption process can be – it was far more in-depth than I had anticipated. But I soon discovered that their slow and meticulous approach was entirely for the dogs' benefit, not their own. Now, having seen how difficult it can be for a dog to readjust after being RTK – returned to kennel – I can understand why the adoption process is taken so seriously.

The rehoming process is carefully tailored to each dog. Each potential adopter is different, so what works for one won't necessarily work for another. This is why the team take it slowly, checking all the angles before moving to the next stage. Occasionally the rehoming process is completed in a few days, but for other dogs, the potential new owners may need to return on several occasions. This has nothing to do with the people and it isn't personal – it is all down to the dog. The carers and trainers need to be completely sure that it is a good match for everyone involved.

When most people arrive at the centre they will have searched online at the dog gallery, which is maintained and updated by the brilliant canine carer Jason. His wonderful pictures capture the spirit of the dogs, and many people will have a web profile of a dog in mind and are hoping to meet that dog. Others are sometimes just there for a look around, and nearly surprise themselves by falling in love with a particular dog.

Regardless, there will always be a member of the rehoming team advising you along the way. If you have successfully chosen a dog, the next step might be to carry out a home visit. Again, this is decided on a case-by-case basis. For example, they might need to check that your garden is suitable to exercise an energetic dog or, if you have another animal living with you, they might bring the dog to your home for the visit so the two can meet. Other dogs require multiple meets at the centre and at home, so the new adopters might have to visit a few times before the process is complete. I know it sounds very time-consuming, but it is simply to ensure that you have made the right choice.

Thanks to all this interaction, by the time adoption day arrives, the rehoming team tends to know everyone fairly well. Before you walk out with your dog, there is the final matter of the adoption talk, where the training and behavioural team give advice about taking on a new dog. It is, after all, a big financial and emotional responsibility, so the team needs to know that the family members are fully aware of the level of commitment involved. A dog needs care for potentially a decade or longer, and every effort is made to ensure that all aspects of having a new dog are covered and any questions or concerns are fully addressed and answered.

The vet suite is always busy coming up to adoption day, as they have to make sure all dogs are physically ready to leave the centre. Before a dog leaves, he or she will get a thorough health screening, which includes their vaccinations. The dog will also be microchipped and all the necessary paperwork is prepared. Each dog that leaves is given a bag with all of his/her personal details in it and any advice on food, future care or any medical history.

While all that's going on at the front of the centre on adoption day, there is also important moving and rearranging going on at the back. As one dog leaves that frees up a kennel space, so there is a bit of a shifting around. Some new dogs will be mixed together and then a massive sterilisation and deep-clean of the vacated kennel takes place, in preparation for a new dog to move in and start their journey.

You get used to the turnaround of animals in your care, but it is really nice to spend some quality time with the dogs who are leaving, whether it's a last walk, a last feed or a play in one of the designated gardens. Over time, your heart doesn't hurt so much each time a dog is rehomed.

One adoption day will forever stand out for me. The centre was packed to capacity, as always, and kennel spaces were needed for some urgent new arrivals, so I was spending my last precious minutes with one of the little puppies I had grown really close to. We were in the puppy garden having

a last play, and I was hoping to capture it on camera before I walked him in to his new adopters. When I first met him, he was still quite a young little puppy. He had come to Dogs Trust from a pound with his littermates – a riotous bunch of Pointer cross Bulldogs about thirteen weeks old.

When they'd arrived at the centre, there were a lot of concerns for him as one of his brothers had tested positive for parvovirus, a deadly disease that can be fatal for dogs, so a close eye was kept on the rest of the litter, and especially him. By all accounts he was the runt of the litter, and due to his smaller size he was always competing with his siblings for food, and even attention, when we would go to see them in the kennel. He didn't need to worry as he always got plenty of attention from me, and even a nickname.

My little guy had more than his size as a disadvantage, he also had a large fluid-filled bump on his head, due to the accumulation of serosanguinous fluid around his occipital protuberance, which had to be drained a couple of times during his stay. From an early age I could identify him from the group and I called him 'bumpy head'. Although this wasn't his official name, we all ended up calling him Bumpy after a few weeks.

These thirteen pups were a lively and beautiful litter, and I had the pleasure to be very involved in their care. They were a memorable bunch. On the first day they met me, I had to go into their kennel to pick up little Bumpy – a simple task, you would think. Before I could get to him, his pals were jumping all over me, eating my white protective suit. As I bent down to try to take the little bits of my white suit that some of them had managed to bite off, the others saw an opportunity to nibble on my hair, which was dangling down! I think they thought I was a human toy! By the time I managed to get to Bumpy, my suit was shredded at the bottom and I needed to sit down for a rest. They were full on!

By the end of that day I had bathed them, cleaned them, fed them and played with them. Like everyone else who cared for them, I had fallen madly in puppy love with them all. As predicted, one by one they were all chosen for their forever home – all except one.

Our special little guy took a little longer to be chosen, maybe because of his special 'bumpy head' feature. He was a little different, which might have made some people wary, but it was what made him unique. But then, finally, someone did choose him, and we were all thrilled.

I was excited to be there for Bumpy's last day at the centre. As I waited to be radioed by reception to bring him up to meet his adopters, a few people dropped in to say goodbye. Bumpy had so much personality that Jason came in to take some pictures of him, and managed to capture his personality and his distinctive feature perfectly. This little poser managed to get photographed putting his bottom right up to the camera and turning his head as if to say, 'Does my bump look big in this?' He was an adorable messer!

We all had so much fun with him and, in typical puppy fashion he just jumped around the place, full of devilment and excitement, exactly how a puppy should be! We were enjoying him so much, I forgot about the time, and suddenly realised I should have had him up to reception by now. I radioed them, and was told to bring him up to the front desk. I was getting ready to say my final goodbyes, but when Bumpy and I arrived at reception, I got some very surprising news. His new owner hadn't arrived and wasn't contactable on the phone. It was a no-show.

While we were playing carefree in the garden, the rehoming team was scrambling to find a place for little Bumpy, because his kennel space had already been filled and we were absolutely packed to capacity. Due to his confirmed adoption, there had been some rescues taken in from a pound earlier that day, dogs that otherwise would have been put to sleep. There wasn't room to swing a cat – let alone a dog!

Quickly we were on the phone to our loyal foster carers, to see if they could take him in for a few days. By now it was getting late, and no one seemed able to take in poor Bumpy.

While he waited to find out where he would be sleeping, he was brought up upstairs, where Suzie took him into her office – it was the only dog-free space available in the whole building. Soon it was time to lock up shop, and I was worried about Bumpy. What happened next just showed me the commitment to the dogs from the top all the way down to me, a volunteer.

I ended up helping little Bumpy into the boss's car! We got him some bedding and a crate and he had a temporary home for a few days with the centre's Top Dog. The love the staff have for each animal is just incredible.

The other thing this episode highlighted for me was just how vital fostering is in an organisation like Dogs Trust. For so many people who love dogs but can't devote their time to a life-long commitment, fostering a dog might be the perfect stepping-stone. I hadn't really known much about fostering before then, so I was interested to chat to some of the puppy raisers who support the charity. I was surprised to learn that it's not all cuddles and puppy love, that there is a really vital aspect to the process: as a foster carer, your job is to assimilate each dog to a new environment, which in itself is a tough ask. It requires a lot of organisation, structure, patience and time. In a way, with very young dogs, as a foster carer you are preparing them for success in a forever home, giving them the vital one-to-one connection with people and maybe even starting the training process for the new owners.

Little Bumpy didn't stay with Suzie, his short-term foster mum, for very long as we were fortunate enough to find a new owner for this cute little guy. But when Suzie brought him back into the centre, it was clear to see from her reaction that they had formed a close connection.

I had to ask her: was it hard to say goodbye? 'Yes' was the simple answer. She admitted that she had cried, which was humbling to see, but she said they were happy tears, because her foster pup had found a loving family that he would have forever. As Suzie said, it is so much easier to feel closure when you hand your dog's leash to the new family. She met the new owners and she could see how joyful they were, so it was hard to stay sad knowing he was going to light up a family's world.

And he has! His bump has gone now, and he is almost unrecognisable as an adult dog, but his quirky personality is still very much on show! In fact, this dog could have a show of his own because of all the antics he seems to get up to.

He was adopted during the summer of 2016, during the time of the Rio Olympics, so his new owners called him Rio, and this dog could win a gold medal in mischief. From the moment he arrived he has brought endless fun into the family, and that's exactly what the family love about him.

Rio seemed determined to chew his way through the house on arrival, whether it was his particular fondness for remote controls or his unusual interest in the pointy tips of high heel shoes, there seemed to be nothing he didn't want to get his chops around. Chatting to Dermot, his new owner, it was clear there was never a dull moment with Rio around: 'He makes us all laugh and despite all the things that he does, we can't seem to stay mad at him. We love him so much and he just brings something so special into our family.'

The family had been looking for a dog for some time and, like so many other stories, everything about this adoption seemed like it was meant to be. Children Ellen and Joe fell in love with Rio and Dad Dermot, who is a schoolteacher, described it as being 'so strange … we went to Dogs Trust and he just appeared and everything seemed to just flow after that and before long he was at home.' The lesson here is that sometimes a dog comes into your life at the exact time you need him.

Despite what Rio might chew or dig up in the garden, he has captivated this family and it seems to me that it is that familiar universal story I hear so often: he is the heart at the centre of the family. While they tell me about everything he might chew and ruin, they then tell me more stories of how much love, fun and enjoyment he has brought into their family. No wonder they can't stay mad at him!

Bumpy always had a sense of humor and this is the wonderful paradox about him: for everything he does that makes him naughty, these are the very reasons we love him so dearly. This might seem crazy, but I am sure it will make perfect sense to all dog owners.

As Dermot is a schoolteacher, I asked if Rio had been to puppy classes yet. Dermot shook his head and smiled ruefully: 'My daughter, Ellen, really wanted to go, but we haven't got around to it yet. I know at times he can be a bit of a handful, but it's those moments that I love him even more. He makes me smile when he stares at me with those puppy-dog eyes when he has done something wrong, he just melts my heart.'

It's funny that a teacher was saying that his dog has taught him some great life lessons. 'So what exactly has he taught you?' I wanted to know. Dermot had a list as long as his arm!

Rio loves to play, whether it's running, chasing or jumping, he is always on the go and it has been a good reminder for us all to play and move our bodies a little more every day as well. It is a good reminder to enjoy the little things in life. We all live life so fast that we often forget to get excited and celebrate the good times because we're already on to the next thing. With Rio, we enjoy those little moments of fun daily and as a family I think it has brought us together.

The thing about Rio is he is just so happy to see us all the time. When we walk into the room, the tail is wagging and his eyes light up. When he sees you, no matter what mood you're in, he just runs up and greets you with love.

He is a dog with the wiggliest rear-end and a wobbly run. When he comes up to you, his big paws are up and he wants to give you a wet kiss, it's a tonic for any ill, even if you are in a terrible mood, you can't resist but smile. When he goes down on his front paws ready for fun and games, every stress of the day just fades away and the kids just adore him, he makes us all act like big children.

Maybe we can all learn a lot from our dogs. They are the ultimate dependable friend, and their companionship, loyalty and love are unmatched by any human standards. It's a good lesson for us all to take a page out of Bumpy's book. We could try to be nicer to each other, to be in the moment with each other, to really be present and enjoy spending time with each other. If we could live like that and have fun along the way, that would really be something.

Name:	Skittles
Breed:	Shih Tzu

Arrived to Dogs Trust:

Skittles arrived at Dogs Trust from the downsizing of a dog-breeding establishment.

Dogs Trust History:

Skittles was very quiet upon arrival and had skin issues that required medicated baths. She gave birth to two puppies that passed away shortly after the birth, leaving poor Skittles very upset. Skittles was showered with love and affection by her carers, especially after the loss of her puppies.

When Skittles got over her loss, she showed herself to be incredibly affectionate and friendly with people and dogs. She didn't like to be rushed and preferred nice, slow walks.

Type of Home Required:

Children aged 5+

A home where Skittles will have company for most of the time. A low- or medium-activity level family, preferably with another dog.

SKITTLES
From loss to true love

Dogs come into our lives to teach us about love and loyalty.
They depart to teach us about loss. A new dog never
replaces an old dog; it merely expands the heart. If you
have loved many dogs, your heart is very big.

ERICA JONG

On first appearances, it was clear to me that Skittles the Shih Tzu was in desperate need of care and attention. I met her with Cat, who I was now reporting to daily, and on this occasion I was shadowing her. Cat is the like a canine whisperer, and I was so excited to be training with her, but I wasn't quite prepared for the story I was about to hear. We met in one of the puppy sensory gardens, the sun was shining, and we brought out some blankets, toys and treats and allowed Skittles to wander. Everything was picture-perfect, except this little dog looked so frightened. I wanted to make everything right.

Skittles was a new resident. Sadly, she arrived with a number of other dogs who were by-products of a failed dog-breeding establishment. When the dogs arrived at the centre, there was a concern that they might harbour parasites, or even disease. They were contained as a group in the adult screening area and barrier nursed in order to give them the care they so desperately needed.

Having seen the horrors of puppy farms first-hand, I was all too familiar with the often unhygienic conditions that the breeding mums and their puppies were kept in. Breeding dogs are often permanently confined in very small, barren cages that do not provide sufficient space for the animal. They may never be allowed out of the cage, leading to psychological and medical problems. These dogs bore all the signs that they had experienced a very poor quality of life.

Dogs and puppies are unable to express normal behaviours in that sort of confinement, so it was never just the physical scars that the team were concerned with. Dogs are highly social 'pack' animals and under normal circumstances will be socialised with humans and other dogs from a young age. In breeding establishments, there is often minimal contact with humans, so as a result they can display various negative behaviours, such as fearfulness, anxiety and even aggression, all stemming from an underlying fear of humans and even other dogs.

Without knowing Skittles's exact background, the team couldn't tell what start she'd had in life, but they felt sure that she hadn't been handled before, so they had to build up trust with her.

Like the others who had arrived with her, she was certainly going to be busy with the groomer. Many of these dogs had incredibly overgrown coats, matted hair full of all sorts of undesirables. They also had overgrown nails, and their eyes and ears showed signs of irritation too. Some had more serious medical problems that needed urgent attention, and sadly that was the case for Skittles.

It was clear for all to see that she had serious skin problems, a lot of inflammation, urine scald and skin infections. Many breeding mums aren't bathed, groomed or provided with the most basic necessary care. I listened to her story, and felt so sorry for her. But then things became even more serious when, shortly after her arrival, Cat's worst suspicions were realised. The vet team confirmed that Skittles was pregnant. But she was also severely underweight and totally malnourished. The team had big concerns about her ability to produce healthy puppies.

She was brought into the whelping unit and given 24/7 care, and not long afterwards she delivered two very tiny and sick puppies. They displayed symptoms of genetic or congenital abnormalities, and sadly they passed away peacefully beside their mum.

After she lost her puppies, Skittles needed a lot of TLC. I had met her briefly when she'd arrived in the whelping unit and had seen her with the puppies as I was passing her kennel, but now Cat wanted me to become one of her

dedicated carers and start working one-on-one with her. This is what Cat was discussing with me out in the sensory garden as we watched a nervous Skittles sniff around her new environment. I had lots of questions for Cat, and as Skittles rested gently on her lap in the garden, I asked Cat if dogs experience loss and grief as humans do. I felt sure this dog must be desperately sad about losing her two little ones. In her lovely, caring and soft voice, Cat told me that all dogs need extra attention from the whole team when recovering from giving birth, but particularly following the complete loss of a litter. Cat wanted Skittles to be closely monitored because she might show signs of being upset or depressed, just like a human. Cat felt that, so far, Skittles was doing as well as could be expected. They had limited her activity during the first few days following the loss and just made sure she was in a quiet, comfortable place with access to everything she needed. The vet team were checking her recovery, too, and they didn't notice anything unusual, which was all very positive. So all it was going to take now was time.

I looked at this small, docile and gentle creature, clearly still a little afraid of humans, but to see her slowly moving in closer to us and enjoying a loving embrace filled me with hope. Despite her past and all she had been through, she was still willing to trust us. I felt such anger at what breeding mums are forced to endure in puppy farms in this country. Poor Skittles was so fragile, and I wondered if being in the maternity unit was the right place for her recovery, because there were reminders all around her that new life was being born and thriving.

I was lost in my thoughts when Cat said, 'Okay, I think it's time to get this one settled back in.' We carried Skittles back to the comfort of her lovely bed in the maternity unit. I had to work with the team on designing a diet plan for Skittles. Our VIP little lady, like a lot of the mums, needed a special diet to build up her strength. This meant she needed to be fed more often and with a more nutritionally balanced diet. If we didn't see an improvement, the vet team might recommend special supplements to give her every chance to maintain condition.

Suddenly, over the internal radio system, Cat was called to reception, as there was an urgent arrival. We closed the kennel on little Skittles and I followed Cat to the main area. What waited for us there was a horribly familiar scene, the kind I never got used to during my time at the centre – it always upset me. Sitting in a box in reception was a beautiful black terrier, abandoned, a stray, left all alone and in urgent need of help.

Cat immediately noticed that this newest arrival was heavily pregnant, which I hadn't spotted at first. All I could focus on was her beautiful eyes staring up at me, I felt she was saying, 'Help me, help me'. She wasn't making any noise, just looking up with a look only too heartbreakingly familiar when you've worked with abandoned dogs.

I volunteered to bring her to the vet suite and after a quick examination it was confirmed she was pregnant. While the vets debated about an x-ray to confirm how far along she was, Cat looked at me and said, 'We need to make space for her!'

Things suddenly got very busy. The logistical process of taking in a new pregnant mum means that other dogs need to be moved and shifted on, so suddenly time was of the essence. For every dog that is taken in, one needs to go out, and when one dog could turn into a litter of five or six, the available space in whelping becomes a juggling game. Cat suggested that maybe in a few days, if Skittles was growing stronger, she might do well moving in with a nice kennel friend, leaving her old kennel free. For now, though, this new dog needed to go into isolation, and that kennel would need to be deep-cleaned and apparently that job had my name on it!

It is often during those quiet times of deep-cleaning a new kennel for an urgent arrival that you get time to think and really take on board the enormity of the problem we have in this country. I was sad and emotional thinking about it, and I was unable to control my emotions and began to cry.

I was thinking about Skittles, and her recent loss. Unknown to many around me, I was feeling particularly vulnerable at that time too. I'd had my own hidden battles with conceiving over the years and privately I longed to become a mum again. I felt so bonded to all mums, even canine mums, and after seeing the sadness in little Skittles's eyes, I connected with her pain. I felt she was grieving. I had dealt with the horror of losing a pregnancy, and I wanted to help and support her. Tears rolled down my cheeks as I deep-cleaned the kennel, and my thoughts wandered to the newest arrival, weak and unwell, just like Skittles had been a few weeks earlier. Would she be strong enough to give birth to healthy pups?

How could a dog find herself all alone in a box and, for whatever reason, dumped on the door of Dogs Trust at her most vulnerable moment? I wanted to do everything I could to help. I knew, of course, that I couldn't do anything specifically as nature is nature, but if I could help, I wanted to. Time would tell what would happen to her, but for now I had no time to waste – I needed to finish my deep-clean and make her bed comfortable and help settle her in. I wiped away my tears and got to work.

I did connect with the small black terrier. She was a now named Paris and she was super-friendly and once again the process of her care began. Unlike Skittles, I was with her pretty much all the way through the process, keeping a watchful eye and spending as much time as I could getting a few extra kennel cuddles. In fairness to this little doggy, she was in the best place possible to have her babies. The specially designed whelping kennels have underground heating to prevent the puppies from getting cold. A nice bed is set up like a whelping box, which is big enough to allow the dog to stretch out easily with her puppies when they arrive. We didn't have to wait too long.

I was hoping to be present for the birth. I had joked with her (in private, of course) that I would be her birthing partner, but Paris clearly had other ideas. This little dog was a lot stronger than anyone expected and she delivered seven healthy, strong, adorable little puppies pretty much without anyone's help. It was nothing short of a miracle seeing her with the tiniest and newest arrivals in the unit. She was very popular and lots of the staff popped by to take a peek.

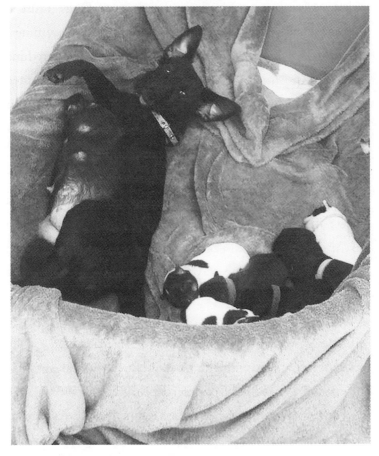

I would often go into the kennel to check that both Paris and her little ones were doing okay. Each time I entered the kennel, Paris would let me know that she was watching me too, making sure all her young were safe. She became quite feisty and protective at this time; her nurturing maternal instincts kicked in, and mine did too. She was very used to me now and she trusted me, a bond had grown between us and I was so proud of her. She was a great mum, always diligently nursing her young.

Soon I was to get hands-on with these tiny little things. At the time, they were probably the youngest puppies I had ever handled. I was asked to administer a little syringe with their vitamins and minerals. It was a big honour, and I was so nervous holding these tiny balls of fur. I had to gently open the little mouths and make sure all of the important liquid was ingested. I think I was shaking a little as I did it and it was captured on cameras for the show. It was so emotional for everyone. I shed a little tear on camera; watching this little dog nursing her young had a deep effect on me. Deep down, I hoped I would become a mum again.

All the time I spent with Paris always made me think of little Skittles and how things had been different for her. I couldn't help remembering seeing her trying to nurse her little ones before they died, and I wondered did she have an instinctive understanding that it was nature's way of ensuring only healthy, viable puppies survived. Her resilience would give me strength during my own time of need only a few weeks later. I felt we had all shared something so special during those first weeks of my training as I too had found out during this time that I was in the very early stages of pregnancy and this bonded me to these two mums even more. It was something I kept private but it made me more determined to help these two mums thrive as I hoped this pregnancy would for me.

Sweet little Skittles had become even sweeter with the arrival of a lovely new kennel pal called Smarties, who was one of the more confident doggies from the group that came in from the puppy farm. In a few short weeks, Skittles had made a remarkable recovery and treatment for her skin condition and other health concerns was going to plan. In the meantime, other plans were being made for her future. The decision was made to get her spayed when she was recovered and well again. This made sense as it would prevent an unwanted litter and ensure she wouldn't find herself in the same situation again.

It wasn't a perfect love story for little Skittles. She had a few false starts on being rehomed and, sadly, things didn't seem to be moving in the right direction for her. Even her little kennel mate, Smarties, had been chosen to be adopted and was now happily living with a new family. Skittles wasn't that lucky – at least, not yet. She was now living with the remaining dogs from the puppy farm.

Paris, on the other hand, had done a great job nurturing her young. Her puppies grew strong and curious and were ready to stand on their own four paws. This growing independence allowed mum some time to meet some of the other canine pals who also called Dogs Trust their temporary home. She had only just arrived when she had her little ones, so she hadn't had a chance to enjoy the lovely fields or runs the facility has to offer. Once she got that chance, she loved it. Soon Paris herself would be ready to go to the rehoming corridor. Paris turned out to be the perfect match for an elderly couple who really wanted a soft dog. I don't know if they found her or if she found them, but either way, I am very glad that they found each other

Paris was perfect for them because of her nurturing nature – she is a carer, and very happy in that role, Paris loved everyone, old and young, and was great with other dogs too. She was one of the nicest dogs you could ever meet, just a gentle, kind, soft, loving type of a dog. Her journey through the centre was a short one, unlike Skittles who was still waiting patiently to be booked.

Maybe it is all about timing and maybe Skittles' healing wasn't complete. Health-wise, she was almost like a different dog and no one could understand why she kept getting overlooked. She had put on weight and had become a regular at the doggy salon – a woman after my own heart. In fact, it was in the salon that I usually got to spend quality time with her. I would often drop in and help Sarah, the in-house groomer, while she shampooed Skittles, all part of the plan to help her skin condition. And it was working, as she was looking terrific!

It was during a salon visit that Sarah told me the exciting news: Skittles had been chosen to be a model dog for a photoshoot with the gorgeous Vogue Williams, to raise awareness about the charity. Finally, Skittles was getting noticed! After the pictures of her and Vogue landed in the national newspapers, many potential suitors spotted her. It wasn't long before the phone was ringing with enquiries about this beautiful dog, and not surprisingly, many families suddenly wanted to take her home. However, something unplanned happened one day. Skittles was chosen to be with a new family, but it wasn't a person who chose her, it was a dog!

I always tried to meet the new families of the dogs I had been working closely with, so in the middle of all the adoption day madness, I made some time to speak to the new owner, Marie, and hear the story for myself. She told me they had a dog, a beautiful Bearded Collie who was four years old called Jay. I felt happy that Skittles would have that important canine company, as she had enjoyed it so much at the centre.

It was actually one of Skittles' kennel mates that Marie and Jay had been coming to meet. Marie told me that she'd had Jay since he was a puppy of eight weeks old and he was full of fun and energy. She had felt that, being such a sociable dog, he was missing a canine companion. After consulting her vet, she decided Jay would benefit from a little friend. So Marie had checked the dog gallery online and then come to the centre with the intention of getting an introduction to one of Skittles' friends.

It was a big decision for Marie, as Jay was her family. Jay had been having some tummy problems in the last few months, so she was cautious about the whole process, not wanting to adopt a dog that wouldn't bond with him. After chatting to the behaviour team, it was agreed that Jay should come to the centre to meet any prospective new friend in person.

The dog Marie had earmarked for Jay was a darker haired Shih Tzu. She felt maybe the opposite colouring might be a good match. But Jay had other ideas.

When the time came for this big Bearded Collie to meet the dogs, he immediately bonded with another shy little dog. This is when Marie met Skittles for the first time. It was love at first sight for Jay, and he and little Skittles were immediately inseparable. As Marie said: 'It was instant, they just clicked straight-away, so it was a foregone conclusion that this would be our newest member of the family.' I was thrilled with the match because I knew Skittles would love being around a confident dog, she needed the security and, just like Jay, she needed the company too.

So Marie and Jay adopted Skittles, and the team was so happy to see their once-overlooked girl find her forever home. After the adoption, I went out on a home visit to see how the two were getting on. They were turning heads everywhere they went in Howth on their daily walks. Thankfully, Marie was well acquainted with the groomers, so now Jay and Skittles (now called Jess) have regular sessions to keep their long hair perfectly groomed.

Jay is such a sociable dog, who loves all family activities, so he was the perfect match to train Skittles and get her used to life as a companion animal. She wasn't familiar with the great outdoors, having spent most of her adult life in a breeding establishment, so even little things like grass, sand, water and even the hills of Howth were a big challenge to begin with. Marie, and indeed Jay, put in a lot of time, love and care to ensure that Skittles would grow in confidence, and she did. With Jay's considerable intelligence and energy, he was able to lead by example and he made sure that Skittles settled into her new routine, making her feel part of their little family 'flock'.

It seems it is not just Skittles who is now thriving, Marie tells me. Jay has settled too, and he is so much happier in every way. In fact, Jay hasn't had any trips to the vets with tummy trouble since Skittles arrived, so even that has settled down too. Skittles has been getting regular vet checks and Marie told me that it appears she has some muscle wastage in her back legs, which is common in breeding bitches and the vet reckoned she was seven or eight years old, going on her dental records. She now loves her walks and playtimes in the garden and around the hills of Howth. They have even got themselves a nickname, Little and Large, and you won't see one without the other. Both are happy and healthy and their perfectly groomed hair catches the eyes of many admirers. Skittles has overcome her fears thanks to Jay, and Jay continues to act like her protector and seems more in love with her every day.

While Jay may have chosen Skittles, it seems she has made a mark on everyone she has met. Marie said she has completed her family, and also that her extended family, her nieces and nephews, have really bonded with her. As Marie says: 'It feels like she has always been with us.'

When the TV show *Dog Tales* aired, I was reminded again about that fateful day when those two brave mums, Skittles and Paris, came into my life and heart. So much had changed for us all since then.

Sadly, like Skittles, nature had played a cruel trick and for whatever reason, instead of delivering a healthy baby, I was left heartbroken. I found out just after my filming and volunteering finished that it wasn't a viable pregnancy. My own private road to recovery would be long and unpredictable, but I kept remembering those brave mums and it kept me going.

Sometimes you just have to trust in the process of life and keep moving forward, despite the knockbacks, blindly hoping it will all come good in the end. I remember watching the show thinking how time can be a great healer; knowing how both dogs' lives had changed over the summer months and hoping my life would heal in time too.

I am glad to say it has. There is always hope when you have the unconditional love of a family, be it human or canine.

Name:	Jano
Breed:	Jack Russell

Arrived to Dogs Trust:

Jano arrived at Dogs Trust as a stray. He was in a lot of discomfort and was unable to stand or go to the toilet. Jano received emergency veterinary treatment, including specialist spinal surgery.

Dogs Trust History:

Jano recovered well from his surgery, thanks to the Dogs Trust veterinary team and his dedicated canine carers.

He was a super-friendly little guy who formed very strong attachments to people who interacted with him. Jano was happy and playful with the other dogs he was walked with in the centre.

Type of Home Required:

Children aged 10+

Low- to medium-activity family.

Quiet home with family members who can give time to his recovery and rehabilitation.

YANO
Everything that's broken can be mended

No matter how little money and how few possessions you own, having a dog makes you feel rich.

LOUIS SABIN

It is no secret that we all have our favourites, or soft spots for certain dogs or breeds. For me, it was the dogs who were in pain that I became instantly attracted to, and during my time volunteering at Dogs Trust there were one or two who were very special.

A little nameless Jack Russell terrier came to the centre as a stray on 7 June 2016. He was in a lot of discomfort and was unable to stand up or go to the toilet. After a check-up from the vet team, it was clear he was in need of urgent medical attention.

Our new arrival puzzled the vet team, and they wanted to get a second opinion. It soon became clear he would need emergency veterinary treatment, which meant he didn't have time to settle in as he was immediately referred for specialist spinal surgery in University College Dublin (UCD).

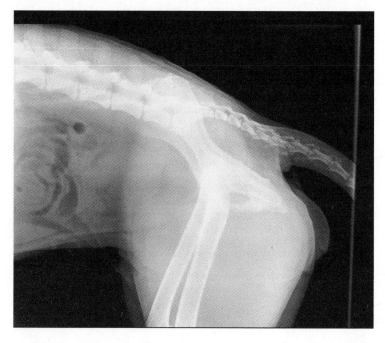

It was a big operation and a tense time for the team as the outcome was uncertain and recovery time unknown. Luckily, he was a fighter and this little dog, now named Jano, began his road to recovery. This is when I met him, and walked alongside him on his journey for a time. He returned to the centre from UCD and was put in the isolation unit, where he could rest and recover. That's where he was when I got a call, along with another member of the team, Dionne, to bring him for an early check-up with the vet. To everyone's surprise, the results were positive and he was doing remarkably well, despite his recent ordeal and the appearance of his spine. His fresh scar looked so massive on his tiny little frame and even the smallest act, like going out to the toilet, had to be carefully monitored. I was so worried in case I did anything wrong and would cause him any more pain, but I had nothing to worry about as the support team guided me every step of the way.

Thanks to the constant care of the veterinary team, the TBAs and the canine care team, Jano got stronger and stronger by the day. He had his daily physio, often outside in the sunshine, and we generally just hung out with him and got to find out a little more about his personality. For a little dog, he had a big heart. Despite his surgery and obvious discomfort in the aftermath of it, he was a really confident and friendly dog who just loved saying hello to everyone he met during his short walks. I was so surprised by how happy he was to be handled, despite his recent operation. Aware that he might be in some pain, we always treated him gently, never wanting to over-stress or excite him.

Over time Jano was gaining strength and more confidence and wanted to play, but this was when the team had to work extra hard to devise the right level of activities to help this high energy little fella get just the right amount of play, exercise and rest. One of my regular jobs was to carefully monitor his exercise and supervise his post-surgery walks and play.

He was constantly being monitored and assessed and it seemed he was really doing well, which was so great to see. He was confident and happy investigating new environments and certainly didn't seem to have any post-surgery pain or long-term trauma. It was agreed that he would be soon ready for adoption and, most likely, would settle in his new forever home quickly!

He would need an owner who was willing to go that little bit extra, maybe not quite a mile! At the centre he was building up his strength and by the time he was ready to be adopted, he was able to do three short, ten-minute walks daily. We knew he had to go to a home that was relaxed and peaceful, with only short bursts of exercise, and that his new owner would also need to be patient and willing to continue his training and exercise routine in his new home.

When they tested little Jano in new environments, he seemed happy. The TBAs brought him to a variety of places around the centre and surrounding areas and he loved it. He was good on his lead and was even toilet-trained, so he was the perfect dog for someone looking for a companion. Due to his surgery, an older household might suit this brave boy as he needed that extra bit of TLC.

Everyone at the centre had fallen for Jano. He was doted on by all of us, most of all by me! Unlike other doggies, he hadn't made many four-legged friends because his surgery meant he had limited interactions with the other dogs. When he was walked with another dog for a short period to assess his reaction to other dogs he was very happy and friendly, but he was never kennelled with another canine pal due to his surgery. Even though he didn't show any guarding behaviours, we felt it might not be good for his recovery if he went to a home with any other high-energy dog.

On paper, it was a tricky ask: a quiet home, no young children, no other dogs, short walks little and often and someone willing to give a lot of time and attention to his ongoing recovery. If we could match all of those requirements, the lucky person would be adopting the most amazingly sweet, loving and caring companion.

A plan was made to give this dog every opportunity to shine and for the right someone to see him! So he was made the Dog of the Week. Every day, Jano was brought to reception and put into the glass kennel that houses the Dog of the Week. The glass kennel is very visible and generally people are drawn to it, which would give Jano huge exposure. Beside the kennel was his card, describing him and his story so far. The first talking point about Jano was his name – everyone read it as Yano, but it is pronounced Hano! He was an excellent Dog of the Week, but when people read about his recent surgery, many felt he might require too much extra ongoing care, and that this would be a lot to take on and a big responsibility. Understandably, he wasn't a perfect fit for many of those who came through the door.

Days passed with Jano being Dog of the Week and while he was getting plenty of attention, there was no real leads for a new owner for him. Like his surgery, he needed a miracle.

Maybe it was divine intervention that brought such a saintly animal lover into his life. Helen wasn't even supposed to be in Dogs Trust on the day she met Jano, and she told me she felt it was a higher power that had brought her there. Helen is one of life's animal heroes, a truly lovely woman who has cared for stray and abandoned animals all her life. She dedicated years to looking after the ones who were often overlooked and told me, 'It is soul-destroying when you realise no one cares, so I had to.' She recalled the first time she took in a rescue: 'My heart literally ached because no one was there for this beautiful old red setter called Rudy. Her owner was old and crippled with arthritis and she was sent to the pound. Somehow I heard about her story and I had to save her.'

She went on to tell me that she and Rudy lived a full and brilliant life for many years. After Rudy died, Helen took in a very sick, old and fully blind stray called Bonny. Her time with Helen was short, but she made such an impression on her that Helen vowed to take in and care for dogs ever since, and she has. She told me stories of all the dogs she had taken in over the years and the lengths she went to in order to give them shelter, love, care and kindness. She became very emotional when she spoke about her last dog, Quince.

Helen told me, 'Quince was a lady, a beautiful Labrador Retriever. I got her as a retired working dog. She had loyally served her blind owner for ten years, until she became too old.' Helen had many good years with Quince, and the dog was in very good health until, almost without warning, she became ill. Helen described how Quince kept making a little coughing noise and although she had it checked out, nothing really showed up. A few short months later Quince stopped eating, and Helen immediately knew something was wrong and brought her to her trusted vet. That was to be her last day with her beloved Quince. The vet diagnosed advanced cancer, and by the end of the day Quince had quickly deteriorated. Helen was heartbroken. Although she had had many dogs before her that had died, she was haunted by the question of whether Quince was in pain for long before she died, and if she could have done anything else for her beautiful dog.

Quince's death had such a profound effect on Helen, she decided not to take in any more dogs. It was too painful, and she felt she was simply too old to do it anymore. She had her loving family for company, her five children, but slowly the lack of companionship began to take its toll. As the months passed, and without a four-legged friend, Helen stopped going out and became withdrawn. One day a good friend and neighbour took action. As Helen described it: 'Divine intervention brought me to Dogs Trust.'

Helen's neighbour had suggested that they should drive up to Dogs Trust, just for a look. Somewhat reluctantly, Helen agreed and they made the journey. Although she told herself she wasn't looking for a new companion, the Dog of the Week immediately caught her eye. She told the front desk she preferred an older dog who would fit her lifestyle, and yet it was this young Jack Russell, with a twinkle in his eye, who put love back in her heart and a new spring in her step.

It wasn't long before he was walking into his new house, and he fit in immediately. Jano was given a chance at a happy life, thanks to the dedication of Helen, who literally nurtured him back to full health. This brave dog's inspiring recovery is a testament to the power of second chances, and his bravery, despite the pain he might have been enduring, inspired Helen to embrace life again and keep going.

Listening to Helen talk about Jano filled me with joy; they are an ideal match. Helen explained that it suited her to go on three short walks a day because, as someone who needed to use a walker, Jano's pace was perfect for her. After their daily walks she might do some training and exercise with him, and then he liked nothing more than sleeping across her lap: 'Look at us now, he is like a new dog and I feel like I have been given a new lease on life too. We are like two peas in a pod and everyone on the road knows me and my Jano.'

Helen had always championed the underdog, but this little dog has become her champion:

He makes me smile, he is so cheerful and always eager to give me a cuddle. He is the first dog to even sleep beside me every night. Time, compassion and patience can go a long way when you are nurturing an animal with a broken back, and as I helped him heal he was helping me heal. Before my heart ached for Quince, and I felt sure I could never love a dog in the same way again, but this cheeky little chappy has mended my broken heart.'

When she said those words to me, it brought me back to a darker part of my own past. I remembered how the grief I had felt for Dad seemed insurmountable, no pill or therapy seemed to offer the antidote to my raw pain. Who knew a ball of golden fur called Dash would come to my aid and be the perfect elixir of life!

Sometimes what is broken can be mended and what hurts can be healed with the unconditional love of a caring soul.

| **Name:** | Kelly |
| **Breed:** | Lurcher crossbreed |

Arrived to Dogs Trust:

Kelly arrived into the care of Dogs Trust as a stray who had been found living in a gap in a wall in Dublin city.

Dogs Trust History:

Kelly was absolutely terrified of people and new environments. It took a few months for her to start to trust people and to get close to her carers.

Kelly's carers brought other puppies to her kennel so she could get used to other dogs, and she did really well with this. She started to grow in confidence and really enjoyed being off lead with other dogs. Kelly then started to initiate play and seek affection from her carers and started to show her funny and playful personality.

Type of Home Required:

Children aged 16+

A home with another friendly, confident dog.

Multiple meetings at Dogs Trust with any potential adopters required.

A home in a quiet area with low traffic. A house with a garden.

KELLY
A lucky escape

A dog is not a thing. A thing is replaceable.
A dog is not. A thing is disposable. A dog is not.
A thing doesn't have a heart.
A dog's heart is bigger than any 'thing' you can ever own.

ELIZABETH PARKER

Being around dogs every day was having a massively positive impact on my wellbeing. I had now been working as a volunteer carer for almost two months. I really enjoyed being at the centre and I was making new friends, both furry and human. I was taken by the love, loyalty and commitment of all the staff to the animals in their care. It wasn't a nine-to-five job by any means – there was no shortage of rescue missions that went on after working hours. I was working with some of the most kind-hearted people I had ever met. These unsung heroes of animal welfare went far beyond the call of duty to rise to the occasion on behalf of animals everywhere, willing to give up so much time to lend a hand to help an animal in need. If there's one indisputable truth that I learned during my time at the centre, it's this: rescuing a dog is the greatest gift a human can give to a dog, and it makes a huge difference to that dog's life. A rescue isn't just the moment when the dog is found and taken into care, it's the multitude of moments after that when the dog is rescued bit by bit – body, mind, emotions, heart and soul.

One new arrival was lucky to make it to the centre at all. Kelly's story tugged at my heartstrings and made me so grateful for the wonderful people I had the pleasure to call my colleagues for the short time I was training with them as a canine carer.

While I was having a morning coffee with canine carer Cheryl, she began telling me about a rescue mission she and some of the team had recently undertaken after work in the evening, in Dublin's city centre. Information had come in from another rescue charity about an abandoned dog in the busy inner city. Initially, all they knew was that this dog was alone, scared and homeless. For many stray animals, finding food is the most difficult part of living on the streets, but luckily for this dog some locals had spotted her and had begun to feed her, but no one had ever really set eyes on her fully. This dog had found shelter in a hole in a wall and appeared to be unable, or at least very reluctant, to get out.

Perhaps, as a homeless dog, she went into the little nook in search of scraps of food, or maybe it was to find shelter from the cold, whatever the reason, no one knew what had led her into a very precarious place. Cheryl and other welfare teams had tried for days to coax her out, but it seemed she had become completely stuck, either by size or fear. It seemed a hopeless situation and no one knew what could be done. One thing was sure, though, they weren't going to give up. After watching the dog for a number of evenings, they realised she would reluctantly poke her head out of the hole for food in the middle of the night, when all was quiet, and then quickly retreat back into her place of safety. With her size growing week by week, they knew they needed to move fast if they were to save her.

Maintenance Mark, as he is affectionately known, had been with the charity for many years, and the team often turned to him for advice. He was used to sorting out unforeseen problems, so when they told him the tale of the dog in the hole in the wall, true to form, he soon came up with a plan.

When Cheryl told me what Mark had constructed, it didn't really make sense. I decided I had to see it with my own eyes, to understand what he had devised. From working with dogs, Mark understood that very often they are terrified of the very people who are trying to help them, and in this case he was correct. This dog retreated when any of the team got near, so Mark's plan was to use minimum human interaction to try to lure this little dog out of her hiding place.

He got a glass panel to serve as a makeshift door. The team attached it to the wall above the hole, securing it with strong supports so that both sides could be harnessed safely above the hole. The idea was that if the little dog did venture out of the hole, this door would quickly come down over it, barring the dog's escape route. The second half of the plan was to make the area around the hole safe and fence it in, so that the dog would be securely outside but unable to run away until they slowly and carefully got their hands on it.

It seemed ambitious to Cheryl, but she trusted Mark's instincts, so they decided to give it a go.

They ventured back into the isolated location, set up the safe area, attached the door safely to the wall above, then left an abundance of tempting food, like hotdogs, chicken and meats, just outside the hole. Then the team moved away out of sight and prepared to wait quietly and patiently.

After a number of hours, when many others would have given up hope, their persistence was rewarded. In the silence of the night, a small shadow emerged, very cautiously, from the hole and they got a proper glimpse of the dog for the first time. She was a lot bigger than first thought. She squeezed out of her hiding-place and approached the food, then began eating. As noiselessly as possible, they slowly lowered the door over the hole. The dog was now contained in the homemade pen.

Mercifully, Mark's plan had worked perfectly. They managed to get close enough to this black dog to make an effective rescue, and bring her back to the centre. As Cheryl told me all this, I could see how emotional it was for her. She was welling up as she relived the story. For her, all those hours of waiting and planning were worthwhile, as this homeless stray was now safely housed in the centre. The lane where she'd been living was called Kelly's Lane, so Kelly became her new name.

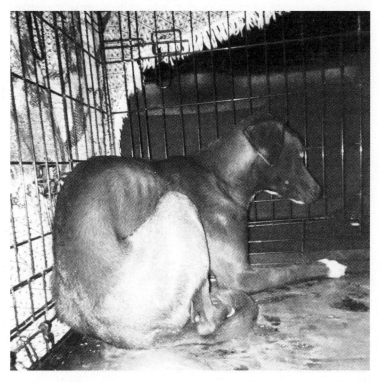

From the moment Kelly arrived at the charity, it was always going to be a very slow journey to rehabilitation for her. She could only work with a few handlers, in order to build up her trust in humans again. The young dog was still very skittish, with a fear of people, open spaces and light. All she wanted was to be in the safety of a dark kennel. In fact, at first they had to create a kennel within a kennel for her, as this was the only way to make her feel safe. Occasionally, she would pop her head out of the inner kennel, or quietly come out for food, but then she would immediately retreat back inside, out of view. When she'd first arrived, she was overwhelmed by all the new sights, sounds and people she was meeting daily, so she was housed in a very quiet and calm part of the centre, to give her time to readjust.

When I began to work with Kelly, at first I would simply sit in the kennel, not moving in too close. Over time I began to put a hand out to offer her food. At the beginning, she didn't budge from the back of her kennel when I was there, but slowly she would come to sniff out whatever I had on offer.

A plan was drawn up for her recovery, and the team went to work. It was a group effort, but with time, patience and a whole lot of love, she seemed to be gaining in confidence with each passing day.

It was a slow process, but I was so excited to see that Kelly was starting to bond with me as she became happy for me to be in her space and started to inch closer to me. During this time, we never filmed these interactions, although on occasion I wore a GoPro camera on my clothing or head. A GoPro is a small box camera that is unthreatening and can be concealed. Her happiness, confidence, safety and ongoing progress were everyone's priority, so a film crew was out of the question.

It might seem hard to believe, but this little dog was afraid of everything, even showing her a collar or a lead was completely worrying to her. So new steps, such as introducing her to another dog, had to be taken in a very measured and planned way. As I learned, timing was key. At times, it was very tempting to move forward rapidly, especially when I was feeling excited about some small victory and progression, but from past experiences the team were able to tell me that you simply can't push a dog too far, too fast. If you do, you risk having to go back to square one and start over.

Progressing in small increments allowed Kelly to feel good about her new surroundings and secure during the process of meeting new people and allowing them to touch and stroke her. After around three weeks she seemed to have overcome her fear of people, so now it was time to see how she would find interacting with another dog. You can never tell how an animal will behave in these situations. If they are nervous, there is always the possibility that they could react badly. A dog's sense of insecurity can be the result of different influences, including a traumatic experience or limited socialisation, like the conditions in which Kelly was found.

The behaviour team decided they would introduce her to a little puppy, under careful supervision. Working with a scared dog can often be challenging and frustrating because they can't tell you how they are feeling. That's why the experts learn to read body language and other non-verbal signals. Cheryl was observing Kelly and her new kennel pal closely, and she felt a puppy wasn't the right match for Kelly as it didn't seem to boost her self-esteem. When describing Kelly at that time, the word 'shy' is an understatement. She wouldn't stand up to meet you, always keeping her

head held down very low and her tail tucked under. She was a very insecure dog, so Cheryl began to think a more confident dog might be more helpful. Immediately, one other resident sprang to mind. There was a lovely, older, self-assured dog in the centre at the time who had been successfully mixed with many dogs. His name was George. Occasionally, George could be little grumpy – like the best of us! – so only time would tell if he would be a suitable match.

Everyone was nervous about bringing Kelly and George together, but luckily Cheryl's instincts were right! George turned out to be a pack leader that Kelly could trust. He gave her confidence, and she even found her voice and began to bark! She started by just copying George, who would bark if he wasn't happy or getting enough attention.

This was a very positive shift in Kelly's journey to recovery. I watched with admiration how the team helped this withdrawn dog to blossom. I learned so much about how to help a fearful dog from my work with Kelly. My instinct in the early days was to cuddle or 'molly-coddle' Kelly when I felt she was nervous, which I read from her tucked-under tail. Instead, I had to learn to ignore this behaviour as she might interpret my molly-coddling as a reward – in other words, she might think she was pleasing me by acting afraid, and therefore keep doing it. So to truly help her along, I had to learn to ignore the fearful behaviour and praise her when she acted with confidence, especially when she appeared self-assured when meeting new people. It was all about repetition and making her feel secure.

Cheryl was following every step of Kelly's rehabilitation with great care, and she decided to move Kelly into a new, larger and more open kennel. Cheryl was with Kelly when they moved her from the puppy screening area to the whelping block. Although this was new for her, and she wasn't expecting pups, it was a very quiet, calm block and it suited this very timid girl.

The next big task was to get her used to wearing a collar and lead, and teach her to enjoy going for walks. She had found a friend in George, but she was still too nervous to leave her kennel for walks, so they had to introduce other dogs to her in her kennel, to get her used to more than one dog. She was slowly learning to accept that humans weren't there to hurt her. She could see the other dogs interacting with the team and watching this helped build up her confidence around people.

So now Kelly was happier around people and other dogs, which meant she was ready to take on walks. She had grown used to her collar, but the lead was a different matter. Every time it was attached, she was very uncomfortable. They tried lots of different ways to help her with her worries around the lead by attaching toys to it, using long lines, feeding her treats when they put it on. It took a lot of time, but they wanted her to have a positive association with this new addition to her training. Everyone could see she was very suspicious of it for quite a while, and many

began to wonder if this very shut-down dog could make the transition out of the only safe space she knew – her kennel.

Eventually, with a lot of persistence, love and patience from her carers, Kelly was comfortable enough to attach a long line. And so began her free runs. It was obvious from the start that Kelly was very doggy social, she loved being out in the field with other dogs, sometimes up to ten at a time. And as each dog has a carer with them, that meant lots of new faces in the field, too. I was there one day with many of the team, and they were all fantastic with her.

In those early days Kelly needed the safety of a confident pack of dogs, and it was so rewarding and wonderful to see her beginning to act like a dog and enjoy the simple pleasures, like a run in the long grass and a play around with other furry friends.

Amidst all the heartbreaking stories that I heard daily at the centre, seeing a dog change from scared to happy was the greatest joy. It made absolutely everything worthwhile. Kelly had arrived to us as a petrified little bag of bones, and now here she was, rollicking in the meadow fields, barking and engaging in rough-and-tumble with her new friends. It made my heart ache with delight to see it. It was clear to see she was on the road to a happier, healthier and more fulfilling future.

Unlike other dogs in the team's care, Kelly took a long time to gain confidence and trust the people committed to her rehabilitation. They took great care of her, because everyone had been affected by the state she was found in:

her spirit broken from months of neglect, and possibly abuse. When she'd arrived, it was clear that something or someone had made her very scared, so the team worked with huge patience, giving Kelly the time she needed to emerge from the darkness of her past into the light of her future. When she did, her transformation was illuminating for all to see. It was a hugely satisfying success story for the whole team.

I couldn't get Kelly's sweet little face out of my head and even after my time volunteering came to an end, I kept in constant contact with Cheryl and asked for pictures and videos to see how this dog was growing in joy and happiness with every passing week.

Eventually, after more months of dedicated care by the team, I got the message I had been hoping to hear for so long: Cheryl let me know that Kelly had been moved to the rehoming corridor with one of her kennel buddies. She was still a little shy and somewhat apprehensive about the big world that she was being introduced to, but she had grown a lot in confidence. She was, in short, a different dog.

Once again, Cheryl went above and beyond to prepare this doggy for her next big adventure. She decided to bring her home for a sleepover to her own house, to see how Kelly would cope with a new environment. As expected, Kelly was very nervous in the car on the journey to Cheryl's home. Once there, she had to meet Cheryl's two dogs, which in fact gave her some comfort. Before long I was sent a picture of her lying happily in a cosy spot on the sofa, and that's where she slept for the evening. Not surprisingly, Cheryl's family instantly fell for her, and they discussed taking Kelly on as their own foster dog, but days later something happened that changed that plan.

Cheryl was called to meet a family in the reception area who wanted to rehome Kelly. The adopters were an adult-only home with a gorgeous Daschund named Frankie, which was a perfect fit for Kelly's needs. The family, along with Frankie, came to the centre and got to know Kelly over a series of meets. From the start it was clear they were very understanding of her difficult start in life. They were patient, calm, caring and always allowed her to move at her own pace. She was soon happy to take treats from them and had lots of fun free running in the field with Frankie, her new pal. And so the full booking was done, and Kelly was ready to leave. The dog that had been so cruelly discarded was finally going to a loving and caring home.

Everyone was delighted, but it was bittersweet for one person. This black Lurcher, rescued from certain death, had bonded so strongly with Cheryl that it seemed her departure would break Cheryl's heart. I was worried she would be terribly upset, but when I talked to her about it, Cheryl said she felt privileged that she worked for Dogs Trust and was happy to play a part in Kelly's recovery and progression on to a new home. As she said, 'Kelly is a true example of courage and resilience. It's an emotional yo-yo working in rescue and, at times, it can break your heart, but success stories like Kelly's keep you going.'

In truth, Cheryl was over the moon that Kelly had found a new home that suited her perfectly, and she hoped Kelly would continue to grow more confident and learn to trust and love her new life. It was heartwarming to hear that the new owners still send in videos and pictures to the team, who love to see her running on the beach or through the Wicklow Mountains with her adopters and her new pal, Frankie.

Kelly came from traumatic circumstances and yet somehow, with Cheryl's (and the team's) help, she learned to forgive and trust again. As a result, she is now as a much-loved member of a warm and happy family. Working with Kelly taught me a lot about dogs but she also taught me about life, sometimes you have to take a leap of faith to emerge from the darkness of your past. Cheryl never doubted Kelly's recovery and I think there will always be a special place in her heart for Kelly, the dog she didn't give up on.

There is a quote by Gilda Radner that Cheryl once said to me, and it perfectly sums up their bond: 'I think dogs are the most amazing creatures; they give unconditional love. For me, they are the role model for being alive.'

Name:	Fozzy
Breed:	Pomeranian crossbreed

Arrived to Dogs Trust:

Fozzy and her two puppies came to Dogs Trust after the closure of a dog-breeding establishment.

Dogs Trust History:

Fozzy was one of the more confident dogs from the group she came in with and was a good mum to her puppies. After her puppies were weaned, she shared a kennel with other dogs but was a little 'shouty' in the beginning.

Fozzy was affectionate to everybody she met at Dogs Trust but when given toys, she didn't know what to do with them.

Type of Home Required:

Children aged 5+

A home where she will have lots of company. Owners will need to commit to regular grooming.

Gets on with people and other dogs alike.

FOZZY
Fallout from a puppy farm

I am in favour of animal rights as well as human rights.
That is the way of a whole human being.

ABRAHAM LINCOLN

I love my dog. I began to hug Dash just a little tighter and appreciate him a little longer after one particular long summer's day at work. I had come home exhausted and despite thinking I had seen it all, I was a little shocked, and mostly angry, by what had happened that day.

Ireland is known as the puppy farming capital of Europe, and the sad reality is we seldom talk about these dogs, who are effectively breeding machines, locked away in shocking conditions, often in darkness. They are left without positive human interaction or socialisation, churning out litter after litter for years on end, and then callously discarded when they get too old. I have seen first-hand the extreme and unnecessary suffering these dogs are subjected too, often for a considerable length of time. In fact, some dogs will be born and will die on a puppy farm.

Why do people do this? You can probably guess – money. The dog-breeding industry is worth an estimated €350 million a year in Ireland. And yet in 2016 only an estimated €95,000 was collected in registration fees (source: Maureen O'Sullivan, Independent TD, *The Irish Times*, 3 November 2016). It is a sickening business that is fueled by greed, and sadly it is innocent dogs who are the victims. The awful thing is that good people who want to be good dog owners often fall prey to breeders who churn out litter after litter. These dog lovers simply don't know that the person selling them their lovely puppy is guilty of an abhorrent lack of care that can damage, maim and kill the dogs unfortunate enough to live in their establishments.

I'd love nothing more than to take a huge broom and sweep this evil wrongdoing out of the country altogether. It's a huge problem, and welfare charities can only tackle it piecemeal. We got a chance to do just that on this particular day. We got a call to say that a puppy farm in the midlands had been forced to close, and the dogs being removed were in need of urgent care.

Once we received the call, the amount of preparation for the new arrivals was of military proportions and, as always, time was against us. The whole team was called to action. Little was known of the condition of animals we were about to take into our care, so we had to be ready for every eventuality. A local authority was removing more than sixty dogs and over twenty puppies from a licensed dog-breeding establishment, and we agreed to take the most vulnerable:

My best boy Dash, aged 12.

The Dogs Trust Ireland team in 2017 with office dog Minni.

Suzie Carley, John Grogan and me! The author of *Marley and Me* was a guest speaker at the Doggie Doo in 2016.

With her distinctive white stripe, Penny is a familiar face around Dublin city. (Photograph by Fran Veale.)

Des Byrne and Richard McLoughlin bring Penny to work every day at Lotts Architecture and Urbanism. (Photograph by Fran Veale.)

Penny enjoying a 'Paw-puccino' in one of the city's dog-friendly cafes. (Photograph by Fran Veale.)

Best friends Alex and Mark McCallum playing ball. (Photograph by Fran Veale.)

Alex at his new home with the McCallum family. (Photograph by Fran Veale.)

Happy days for Bumpy (now Rio) with Dermot, Ellen and Caroline Forrestal. (Photograph by Fran Veale.)

Ellen enjoying some fun in the sun with Rio. (Photograph by Fran Veale.)

Canine companions Skittles (now Jess) and Jay at home in Howth. (Photograph by Fran Veale.)

Home is where the heart is. Jess, Jay and Marie Campbell. (Photograph by Fran Veale.)

It's never too late to find love. Helen Pollard embraces Jano at home. (Photograph by Fran Veale.)

Kelly at home at canine carer Cheryl's for a sleepover.

Ian and David arrive at Dogs Trust with 67 dogs and puppies after a dog–breeding establishment closed in 2016. (Photograph by Fran Veale.)

Andrea with orphaned Shih Tzu 'Munchkin' after the dog–breeding establishment closed down. (Photograph by Fran Veale.)

Fozzy is unrecognisable – happy and healthy in her new home. (Photograph by Fran Veale.)

In the lap of luxury! Fozzy rests on Lucas' lap in her new home. (Photograph by Fran Veale.)

Fozzy's babies after being rescued from a dog-breeding establishment. (Photograph by Fran Veale.)

An instant connection – Cosmo Corrigan with Aisling. (Photograph by Fran Veale.)

Dogs Trust education dogs Ollie and Jake enjoy a day off. (Photograph by Fran Veale.)

Off-duty ambulance driver Ian and education manager Fiona with Ollie and Jake at home in the garden. (Photograph by Fran Veale.)

Teacher's pet! Kimmie with Orla Gordon at home. (Photograph by Fran Veale.)

Kimmie is happy at last. (Photograph by Fran Veale.)

Claude is king of the castle in his new home. (Photograph by Fran Veale.)

Julia cooks all Claude's meals with daughter Kaya. (Photograph by Fran Veale.)

Andrea and Bruno in Dogs Trust Dublin. (Photograph by Fran Veale.)

Bruno getting licky. (Photograph by Fran Veale.)

Love at first sight for Ted and 'T'. (Photograph by Fran Veale.)

Beautiful boy Ted relaxing at home. (Photograph by Fran Veale.)

Three-legged Mick landed on his paws with the Golden family – Liz, Fiachra and David. (Photograph by Fran Veale.)

Rescued and loved. Mick and Fiachra play at home. (Photograph by Fran Veale.)

the pregnant mums and new puppies. Within a short few hours we had over thirty extra animals in our care.

It felt like this treadmill of unwanted, uncared-for animals was neverending. One by one, litter by litter, all the dogs were taken from the dog ambulance and into the centre, where the staff were waiting to bring them to warm, comfy beds. We worked hard, without stopping for a break, and had soon housed nearly every dog. There were only two more to be brought in, but these were probably the most vulnerable dogs. One was a little orphan puppy, who was, worryingly, alone, despite being very young; the other was a very worried mum with a seriously angry skin infection who was protecting her two young puppies.

I carried in the little orphan, or 'Munchkin' as I referred to him, and one of the experienced carers carried in the frightened mum and her puppies, who had also acquired her skin condition. The canine carers explained to me that although these dogs were in safe hands now, this was still a desperately scary transition for them. They had been moved from the only space they had ever known and transferred on a long journey to a wholly unknown place, surrounded by new people they had never seen before. It was a tricky situation and the dogs could react badly, so every effort was made to ensure their safety and the safety of the staff. Looking into the dogs' worried eyes made my heart sink, thinking of the horrors these innocent animals had endured. And they still weren't completely out of harm's way because their health was compromised and required urgent medical attention.

As always, the vet teams were on hand to give every dog a full health check. There were so many different concerns, it seemed almost inconceivable we would be able to help them all, but one by one we were assigned to different dogs and over the next few days and weeks a lot of time was devoted to nursing these dogs back to full health. For me, it meant doing my first overnight shift with my boss!

Cat lived on-site in one of the houses for staff on the grounds of the charity. Her commitment to the charity was rivalled only by her vast knowledge of all things canine. She remains one of the most committed and caring animal welfare professionals I have ever met, and it was an absolute pleasure to work so closely with her and learn from her. It was a privilege to watch her work and to shadow her. Every time I was in her company, I learned something new about rescue animals. So I was thrilled when she kindly agreed to show me the ropes of the overnight duties.

There are always lots of dogs to check on and plenty to do, but with the number of new arrivals, we had to really work hard. It was during this time that I wondered if people realise just how much love and commitment people like Cat, and those who work at other welfare charities, actually give to the animals in their care. In those hours, when most people were settling down to sleep, I saw her go way beyond the call of duty. It was when no one was watching or giving her praise that I really felt that Cat, and her team, were the unacknowledged champions of canine carers.

While my admiration for Cat was growing, my love for one new arrival was also increasing by the minute. Some of the pregnant doggies were expected to deliver their pups at any moment, while other delicate mums needed an extra helping hand with feeding their vulnerable young. While Cat checked on some of the expectant mums, I was sent in to do a night feed with our little orphan, Munchkin, who was now living in isolation due to concerns that he might be carrying a virus.

It was such a pleasure feeding him through the night, and it reminded me of the many hours I spent nursing my own daughter in the dark hours before dawn. I was so nervous as I tried to hand-feed him, mixing up his whelpy drink, which has all the nutrients he would get from his mum if he were still nursing, and then trying him on slushy solid foods. I remember feeling such pressure to ensure he was feeding, because I knew his survival was reliant on him growing stronger and these night feeds were vital. I was under pressure, but at the same time oddly very relaxed, and it felt right for me to be there.

During the night-shift I got to ask Cat how she stayed so calm despite the vast amount of work and care these new arrivals needed. As always, she was the voice of sense and reason: 'I might seem calm, but my mind is racing to find solutions to ensure we have the right plan in place to safeguard the best outcome for these animals.'

We worked in silence, and I couldn't help thinking that if people were more educated about unscrupulous breeders, this problem wouldn't exist. When you buy a puppy from a puppy farm, that puppy can have a whole host of inbreeding issues, such as deformities or underlying illness. And then there's the common scenario whereby a breeder is left with puppies no one wants, which is when the big problems start. That's when charities, and even pounds, have to deal with the fallout. The thing is, if there wasn't a demand for these puppies in the first place, there wouldn't be a thriving business. People who buy dogs in a car park or at the side of a road are encouraging the underground breeder to keep on breeding, probably never knowing that the breeding mum is living a mostly neglected life in terrible conditions, until she is too weak or old to breed, which is when she becomes some else's problem. Tonight, solving this problem was down to Cat, and how she would help these dogs in her care.

Cat suggested it might be best to try to get some of the arrivals, and especially our weak little orphan Munchkin, out to foster homes immediately, as this would also make room for the new puppies about to be born on-site. She was very worried about little Munchkin. He needed a foster home to give him the best chance of survival, because he required lots of TLC and one-to-one attention over the next vital few weeks. I asked her what she thought might have happened to his mum or other siblings. Cat shrugged and shook her head. These poor pups don't have any records; we cannot be sure what happened to any of them prior to rescue. Once more I felt overwhelmed by the reality of the situation, but I had to put that to the back of my mind because we had more work to do.

Next on our checklist was the new mum with the skin condition and her little puppies. The mum had been named Fozzy, and her two little ones were now called Mary-Kate and Ashley. I can't take credit for those names, but I can for nursing them and giving them their skin ointment. Fozzy was still very nervous, so we tried to make her feel as comfortable as possible. After cleaning her bedding, it was onto the next mum, and so the process continued. These new mums needed lots of extra feeding and care. Infection is always something the team is on the lookout for, especially when large numbers of dogs come in.

Each kennel has its own protective white suits at the entrance for staff to put on. We have to change suit for each litter; when you have seven or eight kennels, you have to suit and boot separately for each one. It's time-consuming and labour-intensive, and that was just our first check of the night – we had to do it all again in a few hours.

I didn't mind, though. I was really enjoying the peace and calmness that came with the night feeds. There was something really magical about being at the centre at night. Most of the dogs were settled in bed for the evening, and I loved walking around quietly and watching them sleep, hoping they were having sweet dreams.

Finally, when we were dropping from tiredness, at 11.00 p.m. Cat declared our shift over and the two of us, who were the only ones in the whole facility (along with the crew, who were quietly filming from a distance). We took a walk through the centre to the reception area to set the alarms, before going back to Cat's house on-site.

The deep silence was suddenly disturbed by the familiar sound of the mobile phone ringing. To my amazement, Cat answered. 'Dogs Trust, how can I help you?' It was an emergency call, and within moments we were quickly walking out to the front gate to help a member of the public who had managed to catch a stray dog who was in immediate danger, wandering near a busy road. We did the only thing we could do – we took the little unfortunate soul in. The next problem was space. Where could we possibly put this latest arrival?

It was a scramble to get new, clean bedding ready and a space for this small dog was found in the holding area of the vet suite. It would be okay for the night, but once morning came the area would be busy with the vet referrals, so he'd have to be moved. We decided to figure that one out in the morning.

There was one final glimmer of hope – perhaps he was microchipped? Cat got the scanner, but sadly nothing was found. All we could do was make him comfortable and wait for morning, hoping his owner would find him via our Facebook appeal and come to collect him. He was in reasonable condition, despite being underweight and having a matted coat. Yet another dog, I found myself thinking, with no information about his backstory, sitting in a kennel, alone, frightened and unwanted. It seemed like an insoluble problem, and I wondered how the morning staff would cope as they were totally stretched to capacity.

Cat and I finally got to leave at 2.00 a.m. to have a few hours' sleep, then it was up again to face into a new day. The morning brought a new perspective and lots of new energy as the full team arrived for work. They never cease to amaze me – every day they are so cheerful, so enthusiastic, and they all seem to have boundless energy. There were so many dogs that morning, all needing individual care, but among the dedicated Dogs Trust staff, spirits were remarkably high.

And then we got some good news that cheered us all on. A foster home had been found for the little orphan. He had been given top priority and this little dote, with whom I was absolutely smitten, was placed into the excellent care of one of the reliable foster families who were always on call for the centre. Most of the foster families have a long history of taking care of vulnerable animals, selflessly taking on and helping dog after dog, often at short notice. I was so amazed by the love and commitment of these amazing people who were willing to take these animals into their hearts and homes and give them a good start in life. So, one little guy gone, and one extra kennel available for our mystery night-time arrival, who was now called Alan after our sound operator!

No one came forward to claim little Alan, and he was put up for adoption. When I next saw him, it was to bring him for a makeover at the groomers. He had gained some weight and seemed to be in good health. The centre's brilliant groomer, Sarah, totally transformed his matted hair, and when she was finished with him, he was looking healthy and frizz-free. He looked like a totally different dog and a very handsome little fella at that. He was put into the rehoming unit, and it wasn't long before he caught the eye of a new family and he left the charity to start his new life.

Unsurprisingly all the puppy farm puppies found new homes. In fact, my little guy, Munchkin, never spent another night in the centre again. Since then, all he has known is a loving family. After being loved, cared for and socialised in his foster home, he was quickly ready to go to his forever family. He was seen by the nation on *Ireland AM*, ahead of the programme *Dog Tales* being broadcast, and an urgent appeal went out for a suitable home for him and some of the other puppies he had arrived with. As you can imagine, the whole of Ireland fell in love with Munchkin, even the *Ireland AM* producer Brian Foley was smitten!

After that, many people wanted to give him a home, but it was Jackie, Michael and their three children, Céilim, Bébhinn and Brógan, who were the perfect fit for this lovable little guy. Ironically, the orphan was about to gain three loving human siblings, and a mum and dad who would dote over the youngest member of their clan. Brógan had convinced her parents that their recent move to a new house with a large garden marked the perfect time to add another member to their family. They knew he was a little weak and would need lots of extra attention, but they were all willing to go the extra mile for this much-loved doggy.

From the moment they met him, the children started to call him 'our little buddy'.

When I talked to Jackie about the impact of Munchkin on family life, she said, 'It is such a cliché, but he is the fourth child in the family, except he doesn't talk back! He has filled our new home with love. Every day, without fail, he is happy to see us. He even waits for my daughter to wake up and when he sees her, he just wiggles with excitement, he is always wagging his little tail.'

We were all thrilled that the puppies found good homes, but often the ones who are the last to leave are the stoic breeding mums who have endured so much. Luckily on this occasion there was some more good news, this time about little Fozzy. A lovely couple who had recently moved to Ireland from Brazil came to the centre to enquire about adopting a dog. They had originally seen another dog on the Dogs Trust website, but once there, they realised that wasn't a perfect match. While chatting to the adoption team, they heard about the recent arrivals from the dog-breeding establishment and were very keen to help the neediest dog from the group. One of Fozzy's carers, Steve, told them about our brave mum, who had looked after and protected her young, but now was alone and needed protection and care herself. However, Steve also described how Fozzy required more care and training before she was able to trust people enough to start meeting potential families.

For young couple Lucas and Carla, they were willing to wait and commit to the ongoing care of Fozzy. It was early days and the team still had a lot of confidence work to do before she would be ready to go home, so they took the details of the couple and kept in touch with them about her progress. They were happy to wait as they felt she was 'their' dog, but only time would tell if Fozzy would feel the same way about them.

She was still struggling a little when I was involved in her care. I can still remember the morning I had to bring her to the groomer, Sarah, who had a special plan devised to tackle her skin condition. I remember noticing how everything seemed frightening to her, from the sound of the water from the shower to the noise of the blow-dryer. Everything had to be introduced slowly.

During those early weeks after Fozzy's arrival, she didn't act like most dogs. Things that most dogs enjoyed, like playing, seemed completely alien to her. She had no interest, she was almost shut down, unreachable. From this it was clear that she had never been handled much and, to be honest, I wondered if she had ever really socialised with people at all.

As we worked with her, it became clear that she did like human contact, but was scared of it. She was curious to go out on a walk, but reluctant to trust other dogs when they came close. Probably most surprising was when we gave her toys in her kennel, and she simply didn't know what to do with them. It was like she hadn't ever seen a toy before. These were all signs that she hadn't had any of the simple interactions most companion animals enjoy daily, which just made the reality of what had happened to her, and so many other dogs, so much more real.

No matter what anyone says, the way these breeding mums are treated is not right. Everyone seems to know this, but is anything really happening to change it?

I was so angry every time I thought about it, but I had to push it aside because it wasn't serving me or Fozzy well. She needed the confidence to go to the new couple who wanted to give her a home, and we needed to try to give her, and them, every opportunity to make this a successful adoption.

Our regular grooming sessions continued and I got to know her more and more. I began to see a massive change in her. I remember the day when she seemed to be enjoying her bath time and getting pampered. Sarah could see it too, and she was thrilled for little Fozzy. As she said, 'This little mummy needs lots of help to ease the discomfort from her skin condition and the baths are working wonders, so if she is happy getting them done, it will build up her trust that the world isn't a nasty place, that some things are nice and we are here to help and love her.'

I had also noticed that Fozzy was no longer barking as much as she used to, and I wondered if she had she been barking in pain. Now that her fur was growing back and her health was improving, she was starting to act like you would expect a healthy dog to act. She was one of those dogs that you wanted to pick up and just cuddle. Over time, she grew to love being cuddled. It turned out this little scared mum was a sweet, loving and very affectionate little dog. She had been such a protective and caring mum, but once that job was done, she let her guard down and seemed to know we wanted to help her and she allowed us to love her and shower her with kindness.

Her new family finally got the call they had been waiting for, and were told that Fozzy was ready to meet them and that hopefully, after a few meets, she would feel comfortable enough with them to begin the adoption process.

When I talked to Lucas and Carla, I asked them why they had chosen this particular dog and also, why they had chosen Dogs Trust. It was simple, they wanted to rescue a dog that needed extra care and attention to make the dog part of their family. Even things like age didn't really matter for them. It was all about choosing a dog who might get overlooked and left behind because it was a difficult match. When they saw pictures of Fozzy, they could see her condition was poor, but looks were unimportant to them. They wanted to make a commitment to her care.

They were, then, taken by surprise when they met her. Her fur had already started to grow back and she looked much healthier. Fozzy came right over to them at that first meeting, and it was then that Lucas and Carla knew they had made the right decision to wait for this little girl. They felt like they knew her already: 'She was so familiar, almost like we knew her for a few months.' Remarkably, Fozzy was very happy to be cuddled by them and seemed comfortable with them from the off. It was the best possible outcome for everyone.

Rescue animals were the only option for this couple, for very good reasons.

With thousands of pets being euthanised in shelters every year, it's more important than ever to consider adoption … we are just so happy with how everything turned out for us. We are so grateful for the Dogs Trust member of staff who took the time to tell us about all the dogs at the centre, not just the ones on the rehoming corridor or the ones we had seen on the website. If it wasn't for her, we might not have little Fozzy in our lives, and that seems unimaginable. We told her we wanted to rescue a vulnerable dog and when we heard her story, we knew she was the one!

Lucas and Carla continued to keep in touch with the centre and when little Fozzy was strong enough, they came back to get her neutered. By the time everyone saw her again, she was unrecognisable. Her skin was completely recovered and any trace of her past had been completely erased. Some things hadn't changed, though, she still had no interest in toys! Her bond with Carla and Lucas was lovely to see. She spent every moment with them because, as Lucas explained, he worked from home so she was most often found asleep on his lap while he tapped away at the computer.

Away from earshot of the behavioural team, he sheepishly admitted to me that Fozzy even shares the bed with them. They adored her and enjoyed spoiling her with affection and care, but he was eager to tell me she gave it back to them tenfold.

Lucas told me they didn't know what age she was when they decided to put their name down for her, it was her story and hearing about her troubled past that made them want to rescue her. In return, she has brought so much more love into their lives than they could have ever have believed possible. Adopters say it again and again: the love and gratitude you receive from a rescue dog is unlike any other. Fozzy is the light of Lucas and Carla's lives, and it is they who feel lucky to have rescued her.

Name:	Cosmo
Breed:	Labrador crossbreed

Arrived to Dogs Trust:

Purchased for €7 and then surrendered at three months of age.

Rehoming History:

Returned to Dogs Trust. Suffered greatly from the fear of being left alone – separation anxiety. This fear manifested itself in hard mouthing, tugging on people's clothing and lying across doorways in an attempt to stop people from leaving the room.

Dogs Trust History:

A specially tailored training plan. Daily training and doggy play dates. Off-site assessments. Muzzle training.

Type of Home Required:

An adult-only home with a family able to commit to training.

Someone home full-time while working on Cosmo's separation anxiety. A quiet home environment.

COSMO
The big friendly giant

Until one has loved an animal, a part of one's soul remains
unawakened.

ANATOLE FRANCE

They say love is always patient and kind, that it does not take offence or store up grievances. Love does not rejoice at wrongdoing, but it is always ready to make allowances, to trust, to hope and to endure whatever comes. Hope and endurance are two words that spring to mind when I think of Cosmo. Just like thousands of single people searching for the one, he, too, was waiting for someone special.

Cosmo was a striking boy and you couldn't miss him when you saw him passing with his canine carer pal, Andy. They seemed to have a strict daily routine and often walked at the front of the building and across the car park. I hadn't been introduced to them formally, but I had seen them around and, drawn like a magnet, I was compelled to find out more about this incredibly stoic and striking dog.

Over time I began to enquire about the large black dog, to find out how he came to be a resident in the centre. Sadly, his story wasn't atypical, nor was it easy to hear.

Cosmo was a Labrador cross who had arrived into the centre at just under three months old. There was no information from his original owners other than that he had been bought from someone for €7. As often is the case, when the puppy started to grow, the family's love for him dwindled, and he was abandoned at Dogs Trust. As he was a young puppy, he was first placed in a foster home while he was getting vaccinated, to make sure he was medically fit and well to live in the centre and be put up for adoption. On his return from the foster home he struggled with being left on his own, even for short periods of time, and this anxiety was something any potential adopters would need to be made aware of.

Fourteen weeks after arriving at the centre, Cosmo was adopted into a busy family with children. At first, things seemed to be going well, but after a time it was clear things weren't working out, for a number of reasons, and he was returned to kennel. This is a devastating outcome for any dog and can have a huge effect on their confidence and behaviour.

It was clear that Cosmo needed lots of help to manage his anxiety. The owners reported that he would lie across doorways in an attempt to stop people from leaving the room. He would chew everything and become destructive when left alone – he had damaged furniture, rugs, and anything he could find. When left out in the garden, he would obsessively dig and chew. His family described being left alone as his biggest fear.

Before Cosmo arrived back at the centre, one of the managers sat down with his family and went through his whole history. This allowed them to formulate a picture of what was happening in the home and this, combined with his behaviour once he returned to kennels, meant they could immediately identify that all of the issues experienced in the home were connected to the massive stress and anxiety Cosmo felt about being left alone. It was heartbreaking to see this beautiful, strong dog and realise how scared he felt all the time. He obviously had serious separation issues, so the team rallied around to devise a plan to help him. It was a massive effort and many approaches were explored, but most of all they wanted to make his reintroduction back into the kennel environment as easy as possible. In addition, he needed a specially tailored training plan that would encourage him to build relationships with people and, equally, to understand that they would come back if they left him.

His carers worked daily on enriching his life through training exercises in the kennel and in the training barn. He had doggy play dates with his pals to maintain his social skills, along with kennel settle time during which his carers worked on promoting calm behaviour while exposing him (at a low level, to ensure they were creating a positive association) to the things that historically would have caused him to become distressed – such as picking up keys, etc. They worked tirelessly at teaching him to relax while they exited the room, building his confidence that they would come back again.

No stone was left unturned as they explored every possible solution to help Cosmo. They assessed his reaction to being left in an area of the centre with a confident, social doggy pal and noted with interest that on that occasion, he remained calm and relaxed. While that was a positive sign, it didn't mean having a doggy pal would solve his separation anxiety. But it was a start. I was once again in awe of the level of sheer hard work and commitment the team gave to this dog, in order to give him another chance of finding his forever home.

Over time he was brought off-site with his doggy friend, Tighe, and monitored carefully by two training and behaviour advisors (TBAs). All reports back were great: he was brilliant in the car and had settled down in the large boot and had a snooze. It was noted that he might need a bit more confidence as on occasion he was still a little worried by people or odd shapes in the distance and would spook and bark at them. However, once he was given an opportunity to move away or, if appropriate, move a little closer to figure out what the 'scary' thing was, he would settle back down.

The team continued to work with Cosmo, until they were happy to declare him improved to the point where he was ready to be adopted by some lucky family. Time passed, and no one fell in love with this amazingly loving, sweet funny boy who adored his friends, both canine and human. There was no denying that Cosmo was an incredible dog, but time and time again he was overlooked.

As the months and years passed, Cosmo was quickly becoming a long-term resident. He had great days, when he would be really settled and responsive to training, and then bad days when he would struggle. The carers kept track of everything in his daily diary and observation checklist, and it was clear from their records that he was inconsistent in his behaviour, and so needed a little extra TLC and understanding.

Cosmo had grown into a strong adult dog, a big, intelligent boy who needed guidance, attention, love and loyalty. Luckily for him, that's when carer Andy took him under his wing. It was obvious to everyone just how bonded these two were. I had often seen them on their usual walks and they made a dynamic duo. Cosmo was a big dog and very handsome, so they turned heads when they walked by. Having heard his story full of disappointments, I really wanted to meet this long-term resident of the centre and find out why he wasn't securing a booking from a potential adopter. I wondered if he was a product of his poor start in life – abandoned at just three months old. It was sad to think that although he had worked hard and made great progress, it wasn't enough. Why was he still left at the centre, waiting for a new home?

I asked if I could be paired up with Andy and begin the process of meeting Cosmo. From his history, I was expecting Cosmo to be a little shy or maybe slightly anxious around me, especially given that the camera crew would be filming us from a distance. Surprisingly, it was quite the opposite. I think I was probably more nervous of him than he was of me. Andy put me at ease, though, and gave me some great advice about lead training and reminded me that the dogs could sense nervousness, so I had to be calm and confident. I did exactly as Andy said, and before I knew it I was walking this strong dog on the lead and he was being very controlled and gentle, not pulling in any way.

We continued to meet for walks and also did some work muzzle training. Like most dogs, Cosmo is kept on a muzzle when walking in common areas of the facility, although it can be removed when we are in the secure fields or training spaces. I was really enjoying getting to know Cosmo and Andy. They were a great pair, with an unspoken communication between them that was lovely to see.

As always, I asked what type of family would suit Cosmo, and Andy seemed confident that with the proper introductions and some time and patience, he could potentially settle into any adult family. As expected, the main concern was that someone would be home with him. In addition, any potential adopter would need to commit to multiple meets at the centre and in their home, working closely with the behaviour team building up to eventually adopting Cosmo. They would also need to be aware of his separation issues and prepared to be with him full-time while working on his anxiety.

Andy was quick to mention that Cosmo liked feline company too, so if the owners had other animals, this would also be preferable, although not essential. I could tell Andy was so proud, telling me how his best buddy had recently been introduced to a cat in a home environment and had coped very well. He had displayed no anxiety while exploring the sitting room of the house and had quickly made himself comfortable on one of the armchairs. He had had some lovely interactions with the potential adopters and was not shy or nervous around them or the unfamiliar member of staff. When the cat was introduced to the room, Cosmo did become nervous and did some spook barking, but he was easily distracted from the cat with the use of hotdogs and treats.

This introduction of the cat into the room with Cosmo was repeated a number of times, and although he did continue to spook bark, each time there were longer periods of the cat being present before the spook barking began. In all cases Cosmo was happy to forget about the cat when hotdogs were offered as a distraction. It was felt that, with work, Cosmo would be able to live in a home with a cat.

For Cosmo, any member of the potential new family and any possible future adoption would have to be managed and supervised by the TBAs to give him every chance of finding the perfect family and avoid being returned again.

Over a number of days I built up a great connection with Cosmo and while we walked and chatted, I found out lots about Cosmo and also about Andy. I discovered that Andy takes a special interest in the long-term residents of the centre because he, too, is a long-termer – he has been with the charity since it opened in 2009 and is regularly described as being part of the furniture. I really enjoyed working with him as he had so many stories to tell me about the many miraculous transformations he had witnessed among the animals in his care. For this reason, he was always positive. While I was growing worried for Cosmo, fearing he would never find a home, Andy was the opposite, totally confident that 'Cossy' would find the perfect home one day.

I was really struck by the bond between Andy and Cosmo and watching their interactions was a joy. As we discussed his needs and potential new home, Andy turned to Cosmo and said, 'Someone special will fall in love with you, and you will be happy in your new home. It's just a matter of time, buddy!' My heart was aching to hear it, so before I disgraced myself by bursting into tears, I suggested Andy show me some of the focus training work I would be doing with Cosmo. We headed to the field where Cosmo loved being off lead and would run around madly. Within minutes, Andy was showing me the amazing tricks he had been teaching Cosmo. He had even trained him to give hugs, and I got lots of them over that afternoon and over the weeks to come.

Andy explained how he believed Cosmo was one of the most intelligent dogs he had ever worked with at the centre and he felt Cosmo just needed an owner who would be committed to raising a smart dog. Like Cosmo, some dog breeds stand apart from the rest because they are capable of many skills, but without stimulation these dogs can be extremely destructive. Some dogs are happy to fetch a ball, and throwing a ball is enough for them, along with daily walks and physical activity. But others, as Andy explained, need mental stimulation and they suffer from the lack of it. Andy had worked on teaching Cosmo obedience, and had also taught him tricks. He described how much Cosmo relished a challenge, how much he enjoyed those sessions – and of course the results were there to see in Cosmo's behaviour around Andy. However, a new owner would have to be happy to go above and beyond for Cosmo, just as Andy was doing. He needed someone who was going to invest much more of themselves into owning a dog. It would need to be a marriage of sorts!

From my short time working with Andy and Cosmo, I could see why bonding with such an intelligent, committed dog like Cosmo offered a new level of companionship. He was different, there was no denying it. Having a dog that is able to comprehend and follow a number of different commands creates a relationship that is hard to put into words, but I could see that closeness between them when I worked with them. I felt that Andy totally understood Cosmo and that he was right – this dog needed a higher level of commitment to thrive and be happy. But unlike Andy, I couldn't help thinking: was it possible to find that sort of commitment?

Cosmo had been at the centre for three years when assistant manager Catherine made a breakthrough. She met Aisling and her three adult boys, Andrew (15), Peter (20) and James (25). They arrived at Dogs Trust with more than one dog in mind for the family. Everyone had a different opinion, and they all seemed to like different dogs. It was shortlisted down to two dogs, and they were brought to meet them, but Catherine could see neither was a match made in canine heaven. As with all dog adoptions, it has to be right for everyone in the family and, most importantly, it has to be right for the dog.

Just like people, dogs have a unique personality and each one has their own quirks and they won't suit everyone. After a long discussion in which she found out a lot more about the family, Catherine spotted a potential match. She suggested they might like to meet a long-term resident called Cosmo. They were open to the idea, but before allowing them to meet Cosmo, she told them all about his past and some of the issues they were still working on. She explained that he was a dog who needed a little extra in terms of training than other dogs, and that his personality type meant he could be a little nervous and reactive if not managed correctly.

Catherine waited with bated breath to see how the family would respond to all that information. To her delight, they all agreed that they would like to meet him. When they did, to absolutely everyone's surprise, they overcame their differences of opinion: they were all in agreement – Cosmo was the dog for them. It was canine handler Jason who brought them up to the field with Cosmo, and, for Aisling, it was instant – she loved him and felt a connection, and so did the boys. He needed an adult home and with three boys to help with his training and care, there was no questions, no hesitations, it was agreed that whatever it was going to take, they wanted Cosmo to join their clan.

Their commitment level was tested immediately. He was a multiple meet dog, which meant they would have to continue to meet him at the centre until such time as the team felt Cosmo was happy to go home with them. Donna, who is an assistant TBA, began the training and each member of the family was introduced to all of Cosmo's commands. They came to the centre regularly and carried out ongoing training, including muzzle training and lead work. It did take some time, but at the end of the process everyone felt comfortable that the transition from the place Cosmo had called home for the last three years would be smooth and successful. Despite a few tears of joy from the many carers who had a special place in their heart for Cosmo, it looked set to be a perfect rehoming story.

Cosmo's new family still get follow-up visits from Donna and the team to help them with ongoing training. This was really helpful when they started to bring him on walks to meet other dogs. As he had a history of being reactive, they worked with Aisling to make sure he was confident when he met new dogs and new people in unfamiliar surroundings. The training and dedication on all sides paid off, as Cosmo is now a regular on Portmarnock beach and loves to walk among the deer in the Phoenix Park.

When I spoke to Aisling, it was clear she had been matched perfectly with Cosmo. She is a strong woman, who has cared for three strong boys, and this big, handsome and very strong dog was well matched in this home. She told me that, in many ways, Cosmo had brought her closer to her sons as they all bond on the long walks they bring him on. He gave them all a reason to get out of the house together, and she found they were united in their love and care for him, which meant they worked as a team to ensure he got everything he needed. Cosmo's arrival had made them a stronger, more united ensemble. I could see it, being in their company, and I could see how committed they were to his care. I was so happy to see it because that was exactly what the team had said he needed in order to thrive.

I told Aisling that I'd had many doubts about Cosmo's chances of finding the perfect match, but that Andy had never wavered in his confidence that Cosmo would find the perfect family. I asked her why she had felt that instant connection with Cosmo.

Well, he is tall, dark and handsome and when I looked into his eyes, I could see into his soul. I wanted to get to know his personality. He deserves to be loved, we all do, and he is my perfect soulmate!

She then told me his new title was Cosmo Corrigan: 'He has taken my maiden name!' We both laughed, and I thought back to Andy – maybe he was right and dog ownership was a marriage of sorts. Cosmo Corrigan had certainly found the true love he had been waiting for, and I wished them a long and happy life together.

Name:	Ollie
Breed:	Boxer

Arrived to Dogs Trust:

Ollie came from a dog pound in the west of Ireland and had been surrendered by his previous owner due to an illness in the family.

Dogs Trust History:

Ollie didn't make it as far as the Dogs Trust rehoming corridor as Ian, Dogs Trust's Dog Ambulance driver, fell in love with him over the course of his intended route to adoption.

Type of Home Required:

Ollie was definitely suited to a home with other dogs, which was obvious from his friendly reaction to other dogs passing his kennel.

Ollie was quiet in nature, so he needed someone who would give him the time and space to come out of his shell at his own pace.

OLLIE
A story of hope out of hopelessness

*Compassion for animals is intimately associated with good-
ness of character, and it may be confidently asserted that he
who is cruel to animals cannot be a good man.*

ARTHUR SCHOPENHAUER

My job with Dogs Trust was two-fold: I was there to
be a volunteer, but also I had a role as a presenter,
documenting the work of the organisation for the TV
show *Dog Tales*. I had pitched the series on the whole
concept of educating a wider audience about responsible
pet ownership, as well as trying to change the younger
generation's attitudes towards animals. I was very aware that
I had to deliver on both these fronts and not let either one
slip from view.

I had been training with Dogs Trust for four weeks or so,
and most of my training to date had taken place inside the
centre, working alongside the other carers and the training

and behaviour team. I was now comfortable in that role and felt I was holding my own pretty well. But on this particular Monday, I was told that everything was about to change: I was being sent off-site that week, for a slightly different purpose. I was scheduled to go back to school with Fiona Gregan, Education Manager.

Fiona heads up a team of five education and community officers who go around the country's primary schools delivering the free curriculum-linked workshops on responsible dog ownership and safety around dogs. They also work in the community in places like libraries giving free talks to adults through the 'Be Dog Smart' campaign. I thought the change of scenery would be lovely, but we weren't seeing any schools until Wednesday. So today, I was instead going out on a rescue mission to a dog pound.

I had been inside puppy farms and seen animal hoarding situations, but I had never filmed inside Irish dog pounds. Both the ISPCA and the county councils currently run the pounds, and there are over thirty local authority pounds nationwide. Rather than villify them, I wanted to highlight just why they were necessary: because so many wonderful dogs find themselves abandoned and left to die if they can't be rescued. It wasn't the fault of the pound system, it was the fault of irresponsible owners.

The latest figures from 2015 revealed that 13,051 dogs went into the pound system in that one year, with 1,824 healthy dogs PTS (put to sleep). It's a shocking reality, and that's why Dogs Trust works closely with the local authority pounds. Thankfully, each year these figures are decreasing and great work is being done to continue this trend.

When a dog is picked up by a dog warden and enters the system as a stray, the pound has an obligation to keep the dog for five days in case the owner comes forward looking for their pet. But when an owner hands over a dog to the pound, as 3,437 dogs were in 2015, the pound has no legal obligation to keep it for any length of time. The dog could be put to sleep (PTS) the same day. The majority of these dogs are healthy animals surrendered by their owners who cannot, or in some cases will not, care for their pet anymore. This is where Dogs Trust steps in, taking up to 70% of their dogs from Irish pounds. And their message is clear: Dogs Trust never destroys a healthy dog. (These statistics were correct at the time of writing this book. Up-to-date dog control statistics can be obtained from the Department of Housing, see http://www.housing.gov.ie/.)

I knew the statistics and I wanted to make a difference, via *Dog Tales*, by highlighting the reality of the work the charity did on an ongoing basis. However, I wasn't prepared for how upsetting it would be for me to be part of the rescue work of these animals.

It is a complicated and meticulously calculated mission. As dogs leave after adoption day, places become free for new animals to be rehomed by the charity. Dogs Trust puts the concerns of dogs front and centre. They are always trying to help the most needy and they work closely with all local authority pounds, which themselves are trying to make every effort to rehome stray and abandoned dogs. This is central to what Dogs Trust does and one staff member heads up the transportation of these dogs from the pounds. I hadn't worked with him yet, but now I was going to.

Ian Gregan is the charity's dedicated ambulance driver, and every week he travels the length and breadth of the country rescuing dogs from pounds nationwide. He pilots Ireland's only dog ambulance. Today, I was excited to be getting a chance to go out in the ambulance with Ian, helping with the paperwork and the safe transportation of the animals.

Maybe I was expecting Ian to be sombre, but I couldn't have been further from the truth. Despite our early-morning start he was friendly, happy, jovial and ready for the day ahead. As soon as we sat into his ambulance, Ian told me he loved his job – so much, in fact, he didn't view it as employment, but rather as a hobby. As far as I could see, it was a vocation – for him and for his whole family, who also work for the charity. His wife is Fiona, the education manager with whom I'd be working with later in the week. As he spoke with true heart about his work, I was immediately intrigued and wanted to hear more. I quizzed him endlessly on our long trip cross country.

Could you describe a good day on the job?

A good day on the job for me is simple. My van can hold up to twenty-three dogs, each having their own kennel. If I leave the pound with a full load, that's an extremely rewarding feeling, knowing that once the dogs are in my ambulance and within Dogs Trust's care, they are in safe hands for the remainder of their natural lives. Going to the rehoming centre each day and seeing all those waggy tails I've rescued the day before gives me great satisfaction. I know we are doing something really good.

What's a bad day on the job like?

Bad days for me happen quite regularly, unfortunately. I only have twenty-three kennels on my ambulance, therefore I can only rescue twenty-three dogs at a time. I must leave dogs behind in the pound. This is a space issue back at the rehoming centre. For the dogs' and my safety we cannot overcrowd kennels. But I try not to focus on that and remind myself of the dogs I have just rescued.

So is today going to be a good or bad day?

Today we can only take in ten dogs, so you just have to focus on that.

His answer was short and the silence following it was long. My stream of questions was halted by the realisation that we could only take home ten dogs with us. It was a sobering start. I hadn't considered that we wouldn't be able to save all the animals or fill up every available kennel onboard. As I pondered this, I wondered how Ian would choose the dogs, and how he'd be able to leave others behind.

As if reading my mind, Ian answered my unspoken question. He was quick to explain that it wasn't about hand-picking the nicest dogs. All his collections are pre-selected by the dog wardens at the pounds he visits with Sorcha, Dogs Trust's pound operations administrator They look to rescue the most vulnerable dogs who have already been five days at the pound, and therefore at risk of imminent death.

My mind wandered over all this new information and the questions stopped until we reached a small road that led to a familiar sign, telling us that we had arrived at our destination. We parked up and before we went inside, I tried to prepare myself for what I might see behind the doors. I asked Ian about the conditions inside, fearing the worst. Ian was very positive, however: 'Every pound is different and the conditions vary, but they are all clean and the dogs are fed and watered.'

I took one look inside and it wasn't the conditions that struck me, it was the look in the dogs' eyes – something I had seen before and never wanted to see again. Fear.

Ian started his work by taking the most stressed dogs out first, which happened to be a small group of beautiful young huskies; they looked petrified and pretty miserable. Watching Ian work with such gentle care was amazing. Within just a few minutes of kindness and affection, the terrified huskies were transformed. The first one came out like a shivering, cowering animal and after a few minutes with Ian, I saw something change. It was honestly like the dog knew it was being rescued, and there was a sense of trust there. It took just a few minutes to make each dog, one by one, feel at ease.

Before long, Ian was gently settling them into the kennels onboard the ambulance with soft bedding and some cold water. I was in awe and filled with joy watching him work with the animals.

As the rescue continued, beautiful dogs of all shapes and sizes emerged from the pound. I was surprised to see such young, healthy, desirable dogs abandoned and I couldn't help but think how these were the lucky ones, their five days of purgatory over. Destiny was on their side as they were in safe hands now.

As always, a phone call back to the centre is necessary to clarify if, by some miracle, any more space has become available after the weekend of adoptions and new kennel mixes. On this occasion, it was good news: we could take one more dog, a total of eleven.

This time I went inside with Ian and in my head I was expecting barking, yelping, whining, but it was surprisingly quiet. All I could see were little eyes peering out at me from the metal cage doors, innocent creatures sitting on damp, stone floors devoid of the love of a family and left almost without hope. I felt so angry. How could we, as a nation, allow this to continue? We need to take responsibility. I'll say it again: this is a people problem, not a pound problem.

One dog looked a little weaker and older than the rest and I was immediately drawn to him; he was too vulnerable to ignore. Ian had already identified him as a good candidate for the extra space and he called the centre to say he had an elderly boxer as the last dog for the final space available. It turned out he, too, was on his fifth day at the pound. I was very glad he was safe, but we had to leave four remaining dogs in the pound. I cried, it was emotionally too much for me to take in. Some of the dogs were so young and, given the time of year, it seemed likely some of them just didn't sell for the Christmas market – like the huskies, a family of siblings thrown out like garbage. Or maybe some of them were once loved darling puppies who grew too big and, like wrapping paper, they were bought for Christmas and then chucked out.

For our older boxer, I wondered what his story was. He looked like he must have been a much-loved pet. My mind was racing, and I think Ian could sense my distress. On the way back in the ambulance, we travelled in silence for a long distance and then Ian said to me, 'It doesn't get easier, not even for me.'

A silent tear rolled down my cheek and I felt a sense of hopelessness creep over me. The problem was just so huge, and our efforts seemed puny by comparison. As if sensing this, Ian looked at me and smiled. 'How about I tell you a story?' he said. 'About what a difference this all makes, it can change lives.' I nodded miserably. I didn't think it would work, but I was curious about what he wanted to tell me.

Here is Ian's story as he told it to me in the ambulance:

It was November 2014 and I was starting my day in the Dogs Trust Rehoming Centre. On this particular day, I had a full list of collections (rescues) from a number of pounds. As the morning passed I was organising myself for my next collection in Sligo and I noticed on my list there was a two-year-old Boxer dog. I always get excited when I see Boxers on my list. Everyone has their own breed of dog, and Boxers are definitely my breed. But I was even more so excited this time around because my wife and I had recently decided to rehome a second dog. So I was on the lookout for another Boxer.

I met the Sligo dog warden and he helped me with the five dogs that I was due to collect. One by one they came out on the lead, scared and wary of strangers. I quickly assessed each dog and noted any additional information on my kennel sheet before allowing each dog to relieve themselves ahead of their long journey. I then carefully proceeded to transfer them one by one onto to my ambulance.

Then out came the Boxer. He was a small little boy, extremely underweight, and he had lacerations on his ears, possibly from being attacked by another dog in some way. I could clearly see sadness in his eyes. He was not as scared as the others, but he definitely was a little wary of me, although he still came over for a sniff and to say hello. I instantly fell in love, and couldn't wait to get him on board. I honestly knew there and then that he would eventually be coming home with me. His temperament was excellent; he didn't seem dog reactive, which was a bonus. He was saying hello to all the other dogs with a waggy tail. He looked like the perfect brother for our other Boxer dog, Jake, who was a rescue dog we previously *adopted. I was so excited, I couldn't wait to talk to my wife and explain that I had just found our new dog.*

Over the course of the next few hours I had collections from various different dog pounds. En route back to the Dogs Trust quarantine unit, I have to stop to attend to our doggy passengers, and I must give them fresh water and clean up any mess the dogs may make in their kennels. Some of the dogs are not great travellers and tend to be sick. Every time I stopped and opened the side door to the ambulance, the Boxer was always there with his waggy tail. The expression on his face never changed, though, he still looked so very sad. I tried to give him some love, to reassure him everything would be okay, but it's hard to get through to these dogs, at this stage, as they are so frightened and don't know what is happening. What they have all been through and where they have been must have been a horrendous experience.

On arrival I took each dog into the quarantine unit, and I left the Boxer till last. I wanted to spend a little more time with him before he went to his kennel. So I took him to one of the compounds and let him off lead. I played with him for about fifteen minutes, all the while assessing him and his temperament. He was a little gem. I took photos and video recordings of him, to show my wife when I got home. I told everyone I'd be back for him over the weekend and went home to share my pictures and videos of my new Boxer friend.

I was so excited, I couldn't wait to talk to my wife Fiona and explain that I had just found our new dog. She was so excited too and couldn't wait to meet him.

Over the course of the next few days I was in constant contact with his carers, enquiring about him, how he was with his visit to the vets and any procedures he had to go through, was he recovering well, etc. I simply couldn't wait to get the green light so I could start to make my plans to take him home. It took a few days, but once all his vet checks were complete we had already decided to go visit him as a family. We would have to bring Jake, our other dog, too.

I can still remember that day so clearly. I was already smitten, and luckily when Fiona met him, she fell in love too. We played with him for a short while before allowing Jake to come in. At first we kept both of them on lead, but it became evident very quickly they wanted to play together, so, after a good sniff, we let them off, but under close supervision. It was a joy to watch both of them gently running around together, sniffing each other and saying hello. My heart was about to burst. Jake gave his seal of approval, and we had found his little brother. The Boxer was signed over to us there and then, he never even made it up to our main rehoming centre. Like all adoptions, we would have to fill out all the appropriate forms, but for that weekend that was at the back of our minds. He's now our Ollie, and he's the most adorable little boy. He is chilled, relaxed and has a totally different personality than Jake. But together they are great, always willing to play with each other and never apart. They sleep, eat and do everything together.

Ollie has since become a vital member of the family, but also has become a big part of the Dogs Trust family. Fiona was

keen for him to join his 'big brother' Jake helping her in schools so they decided to ask the Dogs Trust Training and Behaviour Advisors to consider Ollie for an assessment. All the education dogs that go to schools have to be suitable, and it was good news for this rescue dog. He passed with flying colours and soon became one of the team, and sometimes he goes to school with Fiona to be part of the education workshops.

These workshops are run as part of the Dogs Trust free education programme, aimed at children between five and twelve years old. As the future generations of dog owners, these children are educated about responsible dog ownership and safety around dogs, which helps to promote understanding about owning a dog. Because of the rescue work I do, I am hopeful this vital work that Fiona and her team do will, in turn, reduce the amount of stray and abandoned dogs in Ireland. I love to hear the stories from Fiona of how Ollie is progressing, he gets to meet all the children that want to pet him through the 'safe hand' method. The children first ask the owner, Fiona, if they can pet Ollie. Then, with permission, they use their 'safe hand', curling their fingers into a little ball for Ollie to sniff before they ask where he likes to be petted. Ollie doesn't mind. He loves the attention. Ollie meets about 12,000 children a year. He loves his day job, he gets out and meets so many people each day and on his days off he snuggles up on his bed, enjoying his down time. We wouldn't change him for the world.

After hearing Ollie's story, my heart was buoyant with joy. I felt I was with an earth angel. Ian and Fiona's own personal commitment to the charity was just so impressive. I felt so much admiration for this incredibly kind couple and their two adorable dogs who work every day, all four of them, saving dogs and educating the nation. It was basically my whole TV pitch encapsulated in this one family – in truth,

I felt they deserved their own show!

I hadn't met Fiona yet and now I knew she was Ian's better half, I was so excited about my training with her and their two dogs. In sharp contrast to my day with Ian, I would be in school, as Ian said, I would be 'educating the next generation'. I joked with Ian that his wife could be making him redundant down the line and he said with a broad smile, 'Well, that's the dream.'

Could the solution be so simple?

Later in the week, I did meet up with Fiona and I went with her on a school visit to deliver the new 'Be Dog Smart' workshop. It was great fun with the kids, and it was so interesting to watch the different reactions to Ollie who was working with us. I was surprised to see that many young children did not always know how to react when they see a dog, particularly if they are unsure or frightened. Some even decided to run away or scream, which Fiona told me was a very normal reaction for a child who is scared. However, this behaviour may be confusing for a dog, so that's why she and the team developed educational programs to dispel the myths about dogs and help promote true understanding about owning a dog. She doesn't just give the workshops to kids, they are for anyone of any age in society – and it is all for free! Her passion for 'Be Dog Smart' is so infectious that I really bought into the idea that, yes, this could be the solution.

There were still the things I couldn't unsee, and so many unwanted, unloved and abandoned dogs streaming into the charity's care every day. As soon as one went out, another one arrived. It did feel at times as if nothing was changing, that we were all trapped in a vicious circle. Since that first pound visit with Ian, I couldn't stop thinking about the dogs left behind, their sad, lost, confused eyes, looking around to be saved. I tried not to think of their reality beyond that point, but late at night, when I couldn't sleep, my mind would wander to what happens next for so many dogs every day in this country. It haunted my dreams, images of corpses, canine lives wasted and cut short because of the behaviour of irresponsible humans.

But then, during that school visit, there was Ollie, wagging his tail after his busy morning at 'work'. His story filled me with hope. When the dark thoughts threaten to overwhelm, I picture Ollie with big bro Jake and their human parents Ian and Fiona, and that picks my spirits back up again, and shows me some light at the end of this dark tunnel.

Ollie was saved, he got a second chance, and because of this incredible dog, children all over Ireland are learning how to be responsible dog owners. I think of what Ollie's future could have been, what it almost was, but Ian and Fiona rescued him and turned it all around. And now it is Ollie who is tasked with teaching our future dog owners to be responsible. As long as there are dogs like Ollie – and owners like Ian and Fiona – there is hope.

Name:	Kim
Breed:	Lurcher

Arrived to Dogs Trust:

Kim arrived to Dogs Trust from a local dog pound and required medical treatment for a hernia under her neck.

Dogs Trust History:

Kim was pregnant and had a litter of beautiful pups, cared for them well and they were all rehomed. When Kim moved away from her puppies, she settled well and really enjoyed her walks. Although Kim wasn't comfortable with handling, she tolerated it, so her carers were careful to take their time putting on her harness. She loved to play off lead with other dogs, but could be quite reactive in her eagerness to play.

Kim was rehomed and her name was changed to Angel. Subsequently, due to a change of circumstances for her family, she was returned to Dogs Trust.

Type of Home Required:

Children aged 16+

Kim would prefer a quieter home environment and younger children would not be able to walk her due to her reactivity, which needs work.

She needs an understanding home where she will be adored her for her kooky ways and a family who is committed to improving her social skills with other dogs.

KIM
Some angels have four legs

Who can believe there is no soul behind the luminous eyes of a dog?

THEOPHILE GAUTIER

I have been working with animals for years and as the old saying goes: don't work with animals or kids! Much like little children, they don't always follow instruction and their attention span can be non-existent. Most don't go where the camera would like them to go, and of course they don't know what light or angle is best to stand in. This can frustrate photographers or the camera person, but in my mind they are the stars of the show. I just follow their lead and we adjust to them.

During filming at Dogs Trust, I was so concentrated on my new and challenging job as a canine carer that, much like the doggies, I ignored the cameras and just focused on my many tasks. As the months passed, I felt I was on a roll and had really found my feet. Like almost everyone else, when I arrived I loved the puppies and although working with them was generally more labour-intensive – like being in charge of a crèche of babies and toddlers – it was so much fun.

I also formed strong bonds with some of the older doggies, they seemed to just paw their way into my heart and really tug at the heartstrings. It was hard not to fall in love every day – young, old, big, small, shaggy, saggy and svelte – they all had their appeal. The dogs were absolutely the stars of the show, and I adored them.

The series was due to be aired in the TV3 autumn schedule of 2016 and I was asked to choose a dog for a publicity piece for a Sunday newspaper. How could I choose? It was like choosing a favourite child; far too difficult. And what made the process even harder was the fact that I had so many favourites! I had a sleepless night trying to think of the perfect dog, one who wouldn't be too overwhelmed by getting their picture taken with so many new faces around them.

The pups had the cute factor, of course, but then, older dogs can be perfect companions because they are much calmer and generally have better manners. Some of the long term residents generally got passed over in favour of pups, but in terms of a photo shoot, I knew a mature dog would probably behave much better. The other thing I was thinking was that older dogs have really distinctive faces. A lot of the OADs (old age dogs) bore the marks of their past lives – lumps, bumps, scars, grey hair, missing teeth, sometimes even missing limbs — but these dogs nonetheless had a certain dignity about them. When I looked into their eyes, I could see so much character. As I lay wide awake, mulling it over, I had to admit that sometimes age was better than youth and beauty.

My mind kept being drawn back to one particular older dog, a striking eight-year-old Lurcher who had been keeping me very busy in recent weeks. She had two names, or at least she did for me anyway. I called her Kim Angel. This old girl put many younger doggies to shame as she had great energy and loved nothing more than a brisk walk. Could she work as the face of Dogs Trust and *Dog Tales*?

Like many of the dogs that find themselves in kennels, Kim's backstory didn't read well. She was a RTK – returned to kennel. She had first come to the charity a number of years ago from a local pound. When she'd arrived she had required medical treatment for a hernia under her neck, a condition that still needed to be monitored, but certainly didn't stop her from enjoying life.

Like so many dogs, she had a tough start as she was in desperate need of care from the beginning. She was pregnant and whelped almost immediately after her arrival, which was very traumatic for her. Kim had a large litter of beautiful pups and cared for them well. Like most mums, she stayed behind in Dogs Trust after her little ones found new families. A big effort was made to find this super special mum a home to call her own. During her assessment, Kim was quite worried when walking through various new spaces, like the laundry room, narrow corridors and new areas. She was also very sound sensitive, listening out for new noises. In truth, a lot of these anxious tendencies were linked to her past, although prior to the pound, nobody knew what start she'd had in life.

Kim struggled with kennel life at the beginning. She was a little fearful of other dogs and her behaviour often became anxious and reactive. Overall, it was felt this was all down to a very nervous disposition. The team knew they had some work to do and so a care plan was drawn up for Kim, with the goal of getting her rehomed quickly. The team felt Kim wouldn't do well in a very busy household, and would prefer a quiet and laidback home environment with a family that would take time to settle her in. A home was found, and she was renamed Angel, but as often can be the case, despite everyone's best efforts, her first home didn't work out. Kim, or Angel as she was now called, was surrendered back into the care of Dogs Trust.

Remarkably, she settled back in well into her familiar surroundings and routine at the centre. With so many familiar faces around, she was gaining confidence in her kennel and enjoying going out for her walks. While she was still very anxious, she was relatively relaxed in this environment, considering how much she had been through with her puppies and living on the whelping block, and then the awful reality of being rejected. In spite of it all, she seemed to be doing okay, although her fearful disposition was a big worry for everyone.

Everyone knew her around the centre, and she turned heads because of her distinct colouring and striking coat. When I started working with her, I was told she wasn't 100 percent comfortable with handling, so I needed to take my time popping on her harness. When we began our first walk together, it wasn't quite what I was used to. She took off on a little trot and I had to keep the pace. We actually jogged across the pathway until we got to the gate of the open field – much to the amusement of all. I think she liked to get to the field as fast as she could in order to avoid other dogs. In the past, she seemed to bark at other dogs that passed by. I must admit, she never did that on my watch, and I found her to be great playing off lead with other dogs. I really liked her and I believed she just wanted to be loved but, like many humans, she was afraid to trust. I began to call her Kim Angel and we began to work together over time.

I tried to build up my connection with her and by doing so I was hoping to build up trust between us. She struggled a little at times. Sometimes it was the first part of the walk that spooked her, so we needed to help her with that. Even if that meant jogging to the field for the first part of the walk, I would do anything to make her feel safe.

Everyone wanted to see Kim do well. It was a team effort on her behalf. The behavioural team had devised a number of strategies to make her a little more relaxed, and every effort was made to make her ready to go to a new home.

She was the type of dog that you actually felt was trying to talk to you at times. I believed she was communicating and that I needed to understand what she was saying. She knew how to use her voice and often became quite vocal when she was unsettled. She would bark at neighbouring kennels or give a loud single bark if she felt overwhelmed. It was her way of telling everyone she wasn't okay.

I wanted to tell her that it was okay, there wasn't anything to worry about. It would take time and patience for her to understand that. Sometimes she would just freeze on the spot if another dog came close. We all understood her ways, but I wasn't sure how I could help her. I wished I could do more for her.

One thing was sure, she loved her creature comforts. Kim was definitely an indoor dog, enjoying nothing more than lying on her bed after a walk. It was during these down times that I really connected with her. I may not have been able to take away her fear, but I could sit and give her my attention and spend time with her so she didn't feel so alone.

I often sat and gently stroked her and felt her soft coat and delicate frame and wondered how she'd got so many little scars. Marks from her unknown past, no doubt – were they the reason she was so frightened? Her eyes would stare into mine, and I wondered what she was trying to say. I told her I was going to let everyone see how fantastic she was, and I assured her that it wouldn't be long before she would have a bed in a house she could call home.

In my heart I hoped that would come true for her. She was an old dog who deserved happiness. Like so many others, she needed a home without any other dog present, so I wasn't a suitable match for her, but I felt sure if people could see the Kim Angel I knew, they would fall instantly in love.

I thought it over for a long time, and in the end I decided Kim was the best choice for the photo shoot. I felt she could make a good job of it, and I secretly hoped that the coverage might lead to some interest in her from potential adopters. I was doing an interview for a feature article in the *Irish Daily Mail*. The team who came to do it were all great animal lovers, which made things easier. I explained to them that Kim Angel didn't like any sudden movements or loud noises as she was a little nervous, and they all understood and were very accommodating.

The morning of the shoot was gorgeous and sunny. I looked very different. My normal uniform of green and black was replaced with beautiful blue silk, my hair was freshly washed and blow-dried and I'd had make-up applied. I hoped Kim would recognise me, so I put on my fleece over the outfit so she could see a familiar colour. I had nothing to worry about, though. As soon as she saw me, she was as affectionate and timid as always.

The sunny weather was perfect for me, but bright sunshine isn't always ideal for photography, so there was a little adjusting and waiting around while the shot was set up. Every effort was made to make Kim feel relaxed during this time. She was so relaxed, in fact, she took to her favourite position: lying down. Rather than stress her out, I lay down on the grass beside her and we took a few snaps. I was really worried that she might get spooked and find the experience a little too much, but she didn't. She was such a pro. Remarkably, she allowed me to get very hands-on and even cuddle her. She actually seemed to like the attention. Like a true lady, she was poised and photographed beautifully for her big shoot.

Afterwards, I did the interview with journalist and dog lover Niamh Walsh. We spoke at length about rescue dogs and the appalling conditions many find themselves in. I told her about the amazing team at Dogs Trust and about some of the animals that would be featured in the show, like Kim. She was my diamond in the rough, I told Niamh, the underdog of the shelter world. Kim was old, she was nervous, she was dumped, she was at death's door while pregnant before getting rescued and then, sadly, she was returned to kennel. Dogs like Kim have the most difficult time finding a forever home. My little angel needed a miracle. She had so much love to share and I knew that if someone could only invest in her and give her the space she needed, she would blossom in confidence.

To everyone's surprise, our picture landed on the front page. There we were together, lying on the grass, in one of the more casual pictures. I was so proud of her, my cover girl! I had high hopes that she wouldn't be waiting long to be noticed – and she certainly wasn't.

One day a young couple walked up and down the rehoming corridor, looking and looking, and Kim was chosen. Her life was about to change forever from that moment on. One of my favourite sayings is that when the student is ready, the teacher will appear. Kim Angel was ready.

Luke and Orla had recently moved into a new house, a house they had bought with a dog in mind. It had lots of space and a secure garden. They both knew they wanted to take in a rescue dog, and an old dog too. They both wanted to dedicate their time to rescuing an animal that truly needed a second chance at happiness. This couple were the best kind of people! Kim had found her perfect match. The paperwork was completed, the home assessment was made, they met Kim multiple times and felt it was the right decision – green light! Finally, Kim had her adoption day and left the centre – and everyone felt that, this time, it was for good.

Orla was a junior infants teacher, and she undoubtedly had the patience and empathy to help Kim settle in. It wasn't an easy transition for the first three months for Kimmie, as she is now fondly called. It is sort of like when little children start school; it's a big change and it takes time to settle and you have to be very patient. Orla's soft, caring way with Kimmie really helped build her confidence. Like a child, Kimmie needed positive reinforcement, so Orla resolved to ignore the bad or anxious behaviour and constantly reward the good. Orla was devoted to Kimmie, and took everything at a pace that Kimmie could handle.

If Kim was an angel, she'd found her guardian angel in Orla.

I asked Orla about the transition – was it very difficult?

Just like being a teacher, it is a massive responsibility taking over the care for an animal, especially one who is a little older and has had trust issues in the past. We both knew that we had to do everything we could to help Kimmie. We both hoped it would work out and, thankfully, it did. And honestly, that first few months of gently allowing her to get comfortable was so important. The time we invested in her at the beginning has paid off in every way. She is an amazing lady now.

It seems you can also teach an old dog new tricks too! With great pride, Orla told me just how Kimmie had transformed. To help her with her anxieties, they got the help of a trainer. They knew that because she'd had a less than perfect start in life and many changes of homes, she felt nervous and fearful. They really wanted to make her feel safe both inside the home and, most importantly, outside, which was when she seemed to suffer the worst cases of anxiety. For the first few weeks she didn't even want to go outside the house, so creating trust and a bond was vital. Orla and Luke worked with Kimmie and they totally understood her. Orla was quick to point out that Kimmie was a good dog:

> *Her anxiety could be seen as dog misbehaviour, but we could see this fearful behaviour happened only in specific circumstances, when we were about to go out or if she saw another dog on a lead, or if someone new came into the house. She was frightened and we needed to help her learn to trust.*
>
> *Like with the junior infants in my class, I tried to create as many familiar routines as possible. Children and dogs love predictability, so we made sure to repeat the same exercises and motions day after day and soon she knew what was happening next and it seemed to make her feel calm. She knew we weren't going to leave her, we always came back home, and a trip in the car didn't mean she was going to be abandoned again. Our routine is predicable, but a regimented dog is a happy dog and Kimmie is now happy. The change in her is remarkable.*

Over time they gradually got her used to the things she was most afraid of – cars and encountering other dogs on her walks. The process of desensitization took several months, but Orla and Luke took it slowly and never forced her. Over time, Kimmie faced her fears.

Kimmie had a brilliant teacher, of course, and there was one lesson that seemed to really help and that was the introduction of 'touch' focus. Her ability to focus on Orla and Luke when she was in situations that made her nervous was the foundation of her success. Orla described how it worked: 'When she was worried, we got her attention firmly on us and she looked to us for guidance. We trained her over time to get her nose to touch our hand, and once she did that, we would say "Good Kimmie" and reward her. It seems simplistic, but often it's the easiest things that works, and this exercise was priceless for us.'

Redirection is a tactic all teachers, and indeed parents, use with young children, taking their attention away from whatever they're focused on and bringing it back to you, so it seemed natural to Orla to do that with Kimmie, too:

It seemed to really bring out the true dog waiting to get out, her inner confidence was released. Very little makes her anxious now and she now associates that lovely connection of touch with a positive reward.

Our goal was to get her to turn to us when she saw something she didn't like or heard a sound that made her scared, and she now sees us as her leaders and protectors. We are here for her and when she puts her nose to our hand, she is going to get something good. She will always get love and acceptance.

Time and patience can heal most things and when that's mixed with love, anything is possible. It was a long journey for Kimmie, but as she enters the autumn of her years, she is enjoying a life of happiness. Happiness just radiates in their home. They say the more you give, the more you receive, and Kimmie has brought so much to their lives. Orla laughs as she tells me that Kimmie is really a Daddy's girl.

She runs to the door every day to greet Luke with a big affectionate cuddle and doesn't stop running around after him when he arrives. She loves nothing more than to cuddle into his lap, and he just adores her in every way. It is a cliché, but we cannot imagine life without her. She makes us laugh every day, she is full of personality and character.

When friends come to the house now, they say she has brought the heart to make it a home. Our neighbours all know her, and we have met so many amazing people because of our girl. The rewards of having her were unexpected, but we feel blessed. We are the lucky ones that she was waiting for us to rescue her.

Seeing how this once fearful, anxious dog has truly transformed, highlights the importance of patience. This really can't be over-emphasised when it comes to adopting a rescue dog. Maybe love and empathy are the cure for practically every bad experience in our past. Maybe all pains and injuries heal with time. Although Kimmie's many scars can still be seen, there is something new and light about her eyes. She has lost the fear, and it has been replaced with a confidence she makes her seem younger than her advanced years.

The universal force of love was all around me on the day I went to visit my cover girl in her forever home. We all have baggage – some carry heavier loads than others, and some have to live with the scars of their past for many years, but Kimmie shows us that it's never too late to start fresh, or to learn new behaviour that could totally transform our lives. Despite being deeply wounded and rejected in her past, Kimmie demonstrated that if you are willing to trust again in love, you can mend a broken heart and learn to love unconditionally once more. We can all learn something from Kim Angel.

The Irish Mail

14 AUGUST 2016

TV WEEK

FOOD
Designer
Cath Kidston
packs a
perfect
picnic

For the love of dogs

**WRITER AND PRESENTER
ANDREA HAYES ON HER
HEARTWARMING NEW
ANIMAL RESCUE SHOW**

36 PAGES OF IRELAND'S BEST TV LISTINGS

Name:	Claude
Breed:	Pit Bull crossbreed

Arrived to Dogs Trust:

Claude arrived to Dogs Trust as a handover from an organisation.

Rehoming History:

Claude was rehomed and returned twice.

Dogs Trust History:

Claude was very giddy and excitable and wagged his tail so much that he injured it by banging it off various surfaces so unfortunately he had to have it amputated. He literally wagged his tail off!

Claude was a slobber monster and would wash his carers with licks. He was affectionate and just adored cuddles. He had a history of becoming over stimulated when he saw other dogs out on his walks. Due to the commitment of his dedicated carers, he could be walked with other dogs, on lead and wearing his muzzle.

Claude loved to play and loved to shred soft toys so indestructible toys were needed to keep him busy.

Type of Home Required:

Children aged 16+

A strong adopter who can manage his size and strength. An adopter with experience of his breed.

A quieter environment in an area that isn't heavily populated with dogs.

CLAUDE
An exquisite conversationalist

Some people talk to animals. Not many listen though.
That's the problem.

A.A. MILNE

There is a place at the very back of the centre where no members of the public normally have access to. Even the canine assistants wouldn't walk through this area in a normal day. It's a block of very large kennels, with access to a large garden or run to the rear.

I was introduced to the reduced-stress kennels by one of the senior trainers, Gemma. They had told me there was a very special dog there that they wanted me to work with and get to know. I will be very honest, I was a little nervous. These new kennels had an air of uncertainty about them. 'What was this block?' I thought, 'Why aren't these dogs on show? And what does reduced stress mean?'

I discovered that some dogs just don't do well in a normal kennel environment, so part of the assessment of each dog is to discover which kennel type or canine pal would suit that dog best. As you can imagine, this can change as the dog becomes more comfortable, but not always.

High stress and arousal levels in shelters can cause some pretty serious behaviour problems. Naturally, this is what we are trying to avoid as the ultimate goal is to make every dog ready to be rehomed. So we don't want to sabotage adoption efforts by making the dog feel additionally stressed. Dogs are assigned to a kennel according to their individual needs, personality and ability to handle stress. Dogs who become agitated in areas of high traffic, daily footfall and additional noise are designated to a quieter kennel area, to the rear of the main thoroughfare, which is a medium-stress area for new arrivals and for those dogs who are more fearful or under-socialised.

You might notice, if you are visiting this area of the centre, that some dogs here have a blanket draped over the top half of their kennel door or across the glass window. This is to give them a break from outside stimulation. If anyone wants to see the dog, they must bend down and meet them at their level. The medium-stress block, which is similar to the main rehoming block, is just quieter.

Then there is the low-stress area.

I wondered to myself about the low-stress area, and why it was outside in its own area. Similar to the maternity or whelping block, it was a stand-alone place. This new wing featured three low-stress kennels. This is where I met Claude, and I don't mind saying it wasn't love at first sight.

Each dog has an ID card on their kennel that indicates what kind of family they are looking for, how much daily stimulation they are going to need and any behavioural issues they may be trying to overcome. When Cat suggested there was a dog here I had to meet, I was keen to get a glimpse of Claude's history and find out why this big guy was in a kennel space all to himself. Why did he have his own self-contained block?

Honestly, I am always a bit nervous before beginning my work with any animal, and I think this is healthy. But I was quite fearful of this new dog. Claude was big, a strong bull breed that slightly intimidated me. However, when I went in with his trainer, Gemma, he was very interested and friendly and quickly any fears I had disappeared. He was very sweet, and we connected almost instantly.

First things first, I wanted to get acquainted with his pad. It was quite a large space and I was both surprised and interested about the thinking behind each low-stress kennel. At the front was his sleeping area, which looked similar to the rest of the kennels. This led to an outside area, again similar to the rest of the kennels, and outside this area also had a door to the main facility and a second door that led to a large garden with different things to stimulate the dog and also areas used for focus and training work. It was a compound of sorts and it housed a grassy area, a sand area, a stone or gravelly space, trees and tubes for learning tricks and agility. It was very impressive, and Claude was the king of the castle, most of the time!

For now it was my first meet and greet, so I was assisting on a 'parallel walk', where I could get to know Claude and what he was like on the lead with a new person.

Everything works like clockwork at the centre and when Claude isn't using his compound, another dog will often get a little break there from the main corridor. So during Claude's walk and training time, another dog will visit his kennel area to enjoy some time exploring his sensory garden and unique space. There was a visitor dog on that day – and it was Cosmo!

I was delighted to see Cosmo again, but for now my mind was firmly on Claude as our walk began. He was a strong dog, and I was worried. I have little upper body strength due to my chronic health conditions, which cause pain and lack of strength in both arms and shoulders. To the naked eye I appear healthy and, I suppose, strong, but this isn't the case. I misjudged my new friend's strength and while being trained on how to walk him on the lead, he pulled too much. I couldn't hold on and I stumbled and dropped the lead! It wasn't anything serious, but I was enormously embarrassed and felt a bit silly. I must say, Claude was not pulling in any strong fashion; I just have a weak grip. Immediately, he came over to me and stood by me until I was ready to get up and go again. From that moment on our bond was sealed. I love loyalty, and this guy had it in spades.

So I took the lead again and we started to walk, and this time I was being told how to handle Claude on the lead by trainer Gemma. I mentioned I was very weak and I wanted to hand the lead back to her, but she told me, 'No – let's go again. This is good for Claude and will really help him with new owners. This time, when he pulls, immediately stop and stand completely still until the leash relaxes. Either Claude will take a step back or turn around to give you focus. When he does, say, "Yes, Claude," and when the lead is nicely relaxed, we can start to walk again.' So that's what we did, and we had a nice, slow walk with this fantastic dog who never pulled on the lead again. He was incredibly gentle and very patient with me.

The type of breed he is means he is restricted under the Dog Control Act in what age person can walk him – for safety reasons, it must be a person over sixteen years of age. He also needs to be muzzled in public. Sometimes these things can put you off a dog, and hearing how powerful he was had scared me a little, but then seeing how he reacted to me when he felt my weakness made me feel entirely different about him.

I went home that night and told my husband all about this amazing dog, so strong, yet so gentle with me. I was so excited about working with him for the coming weeks and, because I was so smitten, I was sure he was going to find a home.

Over the next few weeks our friendship grew. Claude was a bit of a goofy fella and as my confidence started to grow as a canine carer, I began to relax with him and then something amazing happened … we started to have fun! I had been so focused on trying to learn everything I needed to know and trying to do everything right, that I had been missing out on just having fun. With Claude, I learned something not just about my time training at the centre but about my life: I wasn't having fun and enjoying the moment enough. It sounds simplistic, but I had forgotten how to just be silly and playful. This gorgeous, strong Pit Bull, who had really intimidated me when I first saw him, turned out to be the biggest clown in the centre. When no one was watching and when the cameras stopped rolling we just messed around, and it felt good.

You see, Claude knew a secret about me. I am convinced he sensed that I wasn't as well as I seemed, or pretended, to be. Many people can't tell by my appearance that I am regularly in pain or feeling low, but I felt he understood. When I first met Claude, I judged him on how he looked or maybe the breed of dog he was, and I was so wrong. In a similar way, many people see me as healthy and happy, maybe even strong, and they are so wrong. That gave us a kind of kinship.

Most days I would play with Claude in his garden. He liked to chase tennis balls and, like most dog owners, in his garden they had one of those nifty devices that let you throw a tennis ball the longest distance using the least effort. Well, that's the idea. Plus, using the arm of it, you can scoop the ball up without bending too far. This is a very basic movement to do and most people can do it easily enough. But it's not easy for me. My pain levels were pretty high at that time and

I was experiencing loss of grip and power in my upper body and arms, so when I tried to throw the ball, often it wouldn't fire. To Claude, though, this was a great game, and it really helped him focus. Normally I'd feel really embarrassed about this and try to cover it up with excuses, but my new best friend didn't judge me or rush me, he just waited patiently and allowed me to do everything at my own pace.

I remember one day trying over and over again to fling this tennis ball out of the holder, and failing. I began cursing it as my arms didn't want to do what my head wanted it to do. I simply had too little strength to adequately get the ball out, and I was completely frustrated. To make matters worse, we had company: Jason was with us to take pictures of Claude for the website.

Claude peered at me with 100 percent focus, watching the ball, waiting for it to catapult out of the holder. He waited and waited. I got more and more frustrated. Eventually, when I was almost losing patience and about to scream, he did something hilarious. He went down on his front legs in a playful way and then rolled on his back and did that a few times!

I remember saying, 'Oh you think this is funny, do you?' He came up to me and put his beautiful big head into my waist and rolled it around, then he was gone. He was a fast dog, and within seconds he was up at the back of the garden and when he returned, he dropped a different ball at my feet! This wasn't something he always did. He liked his tennis ball and often would hold onto it for a few minutes, so this was a big gesture of friendship. I cried. I tried to pass it off as the sun shining into my eyes, but I welled up and wanted to take him home that very moment.

He had accepted me. He wanted to make me feel okay. That silent act of kindness was the nicest thing anyone or any animal could have done for me at that moment. I was feeling let down by my body and feeling weak, but Claude made me feel supported, his strength made it okay. Something beyond bonding happened in that moment. It was a knowingness between us, and this dog became my firm friend and I his. I couldn't stop thinking about him, and I wondered if he would get on with my dog, Dash, and if I could take him home.

Being with Claude was like free therapy for me. I started to talk to him openly and we chatted away in the privacy of his little apartment. At first, I began telling Claude how my day was going, what was happening with the other dogs at the centre, then I would enquire about his past and ask how such a handsome, loyal, loving dog had found himself in kennels. Over time, almost without realising it, I started to tell him everything about myself and what was going on for me pain-wise. I was worried about my degenerating health but hadn't divulged this to anyone other than my new friend. I felt safe with him, and I knew he would tell me if anyone was near with a loud bark.

One of Claude's special quirks was to sense when people or dogs came anywhere near his pad. He could sniff them out from quite a distance away, and his bark would be a signal for me to shut up talking aloud. I became so close to Claude that I tried to visit him almost every day when I was at the centre, maybe just dropping in quickly to say hello or to have a look through the window, or to put my hand up to the glass so he could sniff me through the tiny holes. It felt good to be able to share my innermost fears with a friend, even if he had four legs and a tail.

I was afraid if anyone saw just how weak my arms were at the time, they wouldn't ask me to do the hard work involved in being a canine carer. There was a lot of cleaning, lifting, moving, running, washing, bending, feeding – you name it, they did it consistently, every day, and it was hard. I was careful and I wasn't able to do as much as most, but I got away with it. And knowing I could confide in Claude if I was having a bad pain day made me feel good.

So my chats with Claude continued, and so did the work of training him and making him suitable for a forever home. One of the key areas we were trying to help him with was how he reacted around other dogs. While his barking to alert me if new people came close served us well when we chatted privately, it was also something that might not help him get adopted. So he needed to address this. To do so, he would have to go on controlled walks where the trainers would introduce dogs, from a distance at first, along the way.

I would chat to him about that, and ask him why he reacted so much to other dogs. I couldn't be sure why, but I felt he was protecting himself and that maybe, underneath, he wasn't as hard as his bark suggested. He liked to roll around and play catch and just be silly and have fun, so I knew he was a big softy, but this important focus work would really help him secure a new home – maybe even a home with a dog – a dog like Dash?

The legal requirement is that any Pit Bull must wear a muzzle when walking in public areas. This was something Claude welcomed and we could put on the muzzle with ease. He was just so good, never any trouble putting it on or off – maybe because it signalled to him that we were going out for a nice walk. A skilled trainer always accompanied me when we did his focus work and walks.

It seemed he had captured the hearts of many at the centre and had strong bonds with many different people. I remember one day I spoke to some of the staff and casually asked them if they ever chatted to the dogs. To my delight, I found out I wasn't alone; many of them admitted to talking to the animals as if they were human. To my amazement, it turned out that this behaviour was far from silly – in fact, it was the exact opposite! Studies have been carried out and an expert in anthropomorphism, which is the attribution of human characteristics or behaviour to an animal or object, has suggested that the science behind why people talk to animals is actually a sign of intelligence. So I wasn't completely daft after all!

On my walks with the trainer, I would always ask about Claude, and one day we chatted about how he came to the centre. The trainer told me that Claude had arrived when he was quite young, around twelve months old. After arrival, he needed surgery because he damaged his tail through excessive wagging. He didn't realise his own strength and badly injured his tail, necessitating amputation. This had been another blow for him, but with lots of TLC he eventually recovered well. Understandably, he had been a little nervous going into the vet team ever since. I felt so sorry for him – my beautiful Claude had endured a life of setbacks. I started chatting to Claude directly on our walks, telling him the perfect owner was coming for him and everything was going to be okay. In my heart that's all I wanted for this guy, unconditional love and affection.

The months passed and the filming for the series continued, and I tried so hard to draw attention to this fantastic dog in the hope that he might capture the eye of someone special. No one seemed to want to take him home, though. It was probably one of the hardest things to deal with – seeing other dogs leave and find a home was wonderful, but it grew to feel bittersweet because each time, I would think of Claude in his kennel, never chosen.

As the filming was drawing to a close, I wanted to make a special effort to feature him, so we took some new photos to showcase this beautiful animal, with the help of digital canine carer, Jason. Everything was perfect: the weather was sunny, Claude's coat was shiny and healthy, his eyes were sparkling, and he had a face you couldn't help falling in love with. His smile lit up the lens and the images looked super. They went out on Facebook and there was a little interest in him, but nothing ever went beyond that. I was convinced it was only a matter of time as I believed firmly that when we showed the work we had done with him and shared his dog tale on the program, he would capture the hearts of the nation.

For some unknown reason, he didn't. I couldn't understand it, but he remained in the centre longer than anyone ever expected. In terms of his behaviour, he was doing really well. His tendency to become overstimulated by seeing other dogs was now under control. He was even able to move down to the rehoming block for a short while, to give him every chance of being seen by the public and hopefully rehomed. Sadly, more bad news was to come – another setback.

On Valentine's day 2017, I got a message from one of my friends at the centre to say that my pal Claude was in surgery. My heart sank – our worst fears had been confirmed. It had been noticed in early January that Claude was quite lame on his right back leg. He was examined and given anti-inflammatories, to see if they would help. They did help him for a few days, but about a week later he was lame again. Claude was also 'toe tapping' when he was standing, which means only placing weight on the toe, instead of using the entire paw.

Claude moved kennels around this time and was very excited to explore his new environment, and it was thought this might have contributed to his injury. Toe tapping is a classic sign of a cruciate injury. Upon being examined by the vet team, the conclusion was that he had a luxating patella (floating knee cap), but it was hard to do any further examination while he was conscious. Accordingly, he needed to go to a specialist practice, so he was sent off-site to Botanic Vets for further investigation, under sedation. The vet team often work with specialist like Botanic Vetinary Practice and UCD when they need expert advice or treatment.

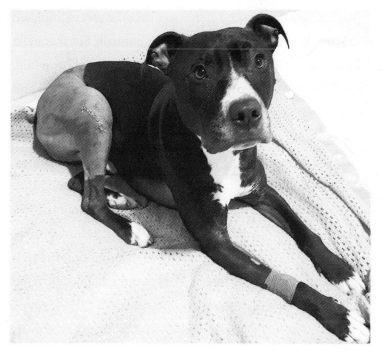

With Claude under sedation, the vets were able to do a cranial drawer test. This is where the vets test the movement of the joint and make an educated decision as to whether or not they think the cruciate needs to be operated upon. In dogs, a cruciate injury usually stems from dogs overexerting themselves, so things like running or jumping excessively in his new environment may have added to this. It was devastating news for everyone. The whole team had worked so hard, and Claude had too, and just as he seemed to be taking a step forward, now he was moving two steps back. The diagnosis was that Claude had ruptured his cruciate, and he underwent orthopaedic surgery at Botanic Vets in February.

Cruciate surgery is pretty intense, so at least six weeks' rest afterwards was imperative. Claude was literally just brought outside for five-minute toilet breaks and then back to his kennel again. He wasn't up for visitors, but I was allowed to drop in one day to say hello. He was back in his old low-stress pad, but restricted to the front part of the kennel only. His recent surgery was obvious from his shaved leg and stitches. I really didn't want to stimulate him too much, so I didn't stay long, but I was broken-hearted and felt like I should have done more, or maybe tried harder to adopt him myself. I was feeling guilty that maybe I could have helped to avoid this. But in my heart I knew our home wasn't right for him. He needed a home without another dog.

For now, though, he was receiving amazing care from the team. He was doing regular physio to build up strength and stability in the leg and, despite appearances, he did seem to be his usual, jolly, happy self, just a little bit quieter than normal. I went up to see him a few times, and I worried constantly about him. What did his future hold now?

But then, the incredible happened. I got word that

Claude was booked for adoption! Amazingly, someone had fallen in love with him, despite his physical weakness. When he was whole and well he couldn't find a home, and here he was, compromised by tough surgery, and now, of all times, someone had stepped forward to ask for him. I could hardly believe it. The new owners had been to see him on a few occasions, to continue the exercises he needed to do daily to build strength. It had all happened so fast I wasn't there on the day he left, but as always the team filmed his departure for his new life, and the video was shared with the carers who didn't get to say goodbye.

Donna, the TBA who continues to work with him and his new owners, gives me regular updates and she tells me he is getting on really well. From what I hear, he is still capturing the hearts of all the ladies in his life. He now lives with Kayla and her mum, Julia, and after a little adjustment period he is now truly settled into his new home and is being spoilt rotten. Not surprisingly, he still loves to play and goof around. As Kayla says, he is known as the bum wiggler – he may not have a tail, but he knows how to shake his booty! And it seems the way to his heart is not with toys or balls anymore, but with delicious home-cooked gourmet meals. Julia, who is an expert in the kitchen, serves him the finest fare every day and her cooking has clearly captured his heart and focus as he waits on her hand and foot.

Speaking of which, Claude still has some medical issues with his legs, but he is being well cared for and is getting all the tender love, care and attention he deserves. Hearing about how much joy he is bringing to his new family fills me with happiness. No doubt his next Valentine's day will be very different for this brave boy. For Kayla, Julia and Claude, it's the beginning of their story together, and I look forward to meeting my friend again soon.

Claude knows all my secrets, and he became my fur therapist while I worked at the centre. I will be forever thankful for his listening ear, kind heart and warm, loving embrace. He never judged me and even on my weakest days he lifted my spirits with his empathy and fun-loving personality. I am so happy he now lives in such a loving home and is being showered with kindness, loyalty, understanding and unconditional love.

I believe in karma. They say you are treated in life by how you treat others; it might take time but eventually we all get what we deserve. Claude truly deserved a second chance and a loving home. His new owners didn't judge him or his ability to bounce back after his illness, and now the support and love he gave me during my low days has returned to him tenfold.

Name:	Bruno
Breed:	Terrier crossbreed

Arrived to Dogs Trust:

Bruno was surrendered to Dogs Trust on 29 June 2014 after his owner passed away in front of him.

Dogs Trust History:

Bruno struggled to get accustomed to kennel life and was a very worried little man. He loves to investigate smells and literally sticks his nose to the ground out on walks. Bruno mixes well with other dogs, even with some dogs who are selective about who they become pals with!

Bruno is very worried by handling and moves away if he thinks he is likely to be touched. He has shown glimmers of the real him: a sweet, affectionate, loving little soul who desperately wants to be loved again.

Type of Home Required:

A quiet, adult-only home with no visiting children.

Owners who will understand that Bruno needs a 'hands-off' approach.

Someone who is home for most of the day and needs a companion.

Ideally, a home with another dog.

BRUNO
All the good ones aren't taken

An animal's eyes have the power to speak a great language.

MARTIN BUBER

I think it's safe to say that any pet owner's worst nightmare is the loss of their beloved friend. Many days I struggle with how anyone can simply abandon a once loved pet so easily; it makes me so angry. But other days my faith is restored and my heart bursts with happiness when I see a happy tail wagging out of the centre, on its way to a new, loving home. Among the best moments as a canine carer are when owners are reunited with their four-legged best friend. There is nothing more amazing than seeing that moment when they lock eyes, and the realisation in the dog's eyes that their loved one has come for them and they are in safe, familiar, loving hands again. It's a special, joyful expression of love. If we could bottle that feeling of happiness, it would be magical.

I have seen an owner come into the centre, clinging onto a dog brush, a lead and some treasured photos, holding out hope of a reunion as they explain how heartbroken they are because their family pet has simply disappeared never to be seen again. Until now, they explain, because a family member spotted a familiar face on the charity's Lost and Found Facebook page – could it be their little furry friend? Their expectation is high, and in some cases, those expectations are realised and it is like a dream come true. There is nothing more satisfying, and emotional, than seeing a dog return to their real home, to the loving family who have been missing them dearly. Such moments drive home what every dog charity wants: a dog in a loving environment.

Home is where the heart is, and when your loyal pet dies, or worst still, disappears, it can be hard to accept they are gone. It can also be hard to quantify just how much of a gaping hole is left in your heart. For non-pet owners, this huge sense of loss might seem strange. It isn't a human gone from their lives, after all. And yet, that feeling of loss is overwhelming when you lose a four-legged friend you have cherished.

When it happens, pet owners are often blindsided by far more grief than they ever expected. I know this from first-hand experience myself. Often people who don't own a beloved pet cannot understand the depth of our sorrow, and that's okay. I work as a Bethany grief minister in my community, and through that work I have supported the bereaved during the loss of a pet. The reality is that it can take months, or even longer, to get over the feeling of emptiness. And I have wondered if animals experience grief in the same way we do.

When I heard Bruno's story, my instinct was that, yes, dogs grieve too. When I met him, I just wanted to help him. So, as I often do with humans who are missing someone special, I just sat with him silently through his grief and pain. Even though he had four legs, not two, I felt his loss, it was palpable and obvious in his eyes. I could sense the great sadness in him because he was missing his loyal companion – his master.

Bruno was an older dog, a terrier crossbreed, and he looked every bit like an old man. He had a few distinct and distinguished black and brown markings that made him very appealing – small, dark and handsome was a fitting description. But he had the saddest eyes. Despite being showered with so much love and care from the team, he looked a little lost. I just wanted to hold him and tell him everything would be okay, in time. But I couldn't do this with Bruno because he wasn't a hands-on dog. If I was going to get close to him and be able to pet him, it would take time.

There was something about Bruno that made me want to find out more about him and the cause of his pain: was it physical, emotional or both? I was intrigued by him.

Bruno had been a very loved family member, but unfortunately his owner died, a death that Bruno had witnessed. This experience was understandably traumatic for little Bruno. A neighbour of the deceased gentleman kindly bought Bruno into the care of Dogs Trust, but had very limited information to give us on Bruno. As a result, Bruno had to have a formal assessment with one of the training and behaviour advisors (TBAs), and the results revealed that this little fella would need a lot of care.

Bruno struggled with kennel life almost immediately, which was only to be expected after his heartbreaking experience. No one knew exactly how long he had loyally stayed by his owner's side or what happened leading up to his owner's death, but when he arrived at the centre, he simply couldn't adjust and relax in his new environment. The canine team noted that he had been rushing people out of his kennel, and almost grumbling at them when they left. He could be exhibiting this behaviour for a number of reasons, although typically it stems from an accumulation of negative feelings, like conflict, frustration and anxiety.

The team of experts assessing Bruno noted that when he entered the training barn for his assessment, he wouldn't settle and would spend the majority of his time pacing the perimeter of the room. Bruno showed little interest in his assessor and was extremely overwhelmed by the room, which was obvious to the team because of his dilated pupils, panting, and heavy footfall. His behaviour became more troubling for the team. The assessor left the room briefly and when she returned, Bruno was hiding beneath a table, crouched down and very worried. After a while, he started to show a little more interest in his assessor and would follow her around the room. His behaviour suggested that it would take him quite some time to settle into any new home. The team felt it was imperative that his new family would work with alongside the TBAs in order to help Bruno settle and grow in confidence.

Often dogs, like humans, can benefit from a good friend, which is why the team always try to find a suitable kennel mate for every dog. Sometimes a confident dog, for example, can really help an anxious dog to settle in better. And so the doggy meets began, and Bruno mixed well when kennelled with other dogs, even the trickier dogs. He was very interested in other dogs on his walks as well, and yet something about him wasn't making sense for the team. They felt he might do better on his own because he was still exhibiting signs of being worried and stressed. This manifested when he was being harnessed, and he still seemed to get worried by handling. Often he would choose to move away from his carers when they got too close, but later, when left to himself, he might decide to come close, even to nuzzle the carer, but unlike most dogs, little Bruno didn't want to be petted. This was strange, as most dogs at the centre craved that love and hands-on affection, but not this guy. It was made clear to everyone that he needed a gentle hands-off approach, and we were all careful to respect that.

Otherwise, he was doing great. He was building confidence with his walks, and for an old dog he was even learning new tricks! He started to come to heel and take instruction on his lead, and after time he was successfully being recalled when off lead! He loved his own company and the chance to potter about on his own, searching out new smells. Most of the time he had his nose stuck to the ground while he followed a familiar trail. Every effort was being made to help this OAD (old age dog) settle. The team were sensitive to this grieving dog and tried to help him cope by increasing the activities he loved to do, introducing toys, more walks, extra play time – anything to help him adjust to life without his companion.

Scientists are still uncertain exactly how pets perceive emotions, and if they are aware of their emotions. Certainly, simple emotions, such as fear, pleasure and hunger, are well documented in animals, but more complex emotions, such as grief and pain, are the subject of debate. When it came to Bruno, his emotional state didn't seem to add up, so the team wanted to investigate more.

This is where Bruno's story really started to resonate with me. In addition to his grief, it seemed there was more pain for Bruno that wasn't visible. As with all dogs, Bruno was left well alone to enjoy his food in peace and quiet, but it was also noted he wasn't to be moved or disturbed when sleeping on his little bed in his kennel. It seemed he liked the extra comfort of a soft area and wasn't quick to get up, like other terriers, for toys or treats. It was all too much effort for him. I could relate to that. Living with chronic pain often meant little movements that seemed easy and effortless actually required a big effort. The team's instinct was to call in the vet experts. Their examinations revealed that Bruno had a chronic condition causing him severe discomfort, and it would need ongoing medical attention and treatment. He was living in pain, just like me.

I began doing parallel walks with him and his dedicated carer, Lynsey. Bruno was now officially a long-term resident. Having been at the centre for over two years at that point, he had his routine. Even introducing him to a new carer, like me, was something we did slowly, over time. At first we both kept our distance, observing each other from afar. I could see that his leg movements looked a bit stiff, just like watching people who have pain issues, I could see he was guarding himself and walking a little off. I am not a vet, so this was more of an instinct than anything else. It is something I can usually pick up with people who have chronic pain, too. We all try to hide it, but there are some telltale signs. He was an older dog, and I wondered what exactly was causing his discomfort.

I needed to know more, so I checked out his medical history. With a seventeen-page file from the vets, I felt Bruno could rival my own pain file from St Vincent's Hospital. I was so drawn to him and I wanted to work with him as I felt sure we would connect. If I am honest, I already felt I could feel his pain, or at least empathise with it. I managed to have a chat with the vets, to get a clearer picture of what was going on inside for this old guy. The x-rays of Bruno's body showed that he had advanced arthritis in both knees and spondylosis, which is degeneration of the discs. I have degenerative disease of the spinal discs and spinal stenosis, so I really began to understand a lot more about this dog's daily struggles. Like me, and many others with chronic pain, his condition was being managed with anti-inflammatory medication. He also had to get regular injections of cartrophen, a disease-modifying osteoarthritis drug that helps maintain joint health and preserves the joint cartilage. Plus he receives a supplement every day to help build the cartilage around his joints. Also, like any human who had the same condition, the team had to keep a close eye on his weight, as any weight gain would put extra pressure on his joints. It became so clear to me why he was worried and anxious at times, and I wished I could take away the pain somehow.

Over time we bonded and to everyone's surprise, and mine too, I was able to be hands-on with Bruno. We even cuddled for a photoshoot and have enjoyed lots of kennel cuddles and special time together. I can almost tell when he is having a good day by his movements. Like anyone living with pain, some days are better than others. The team are so good with him, the care he receives is amazing, and he enjoys his life at the centre.

Despite my heart wanting to make everything okay for him, my head was telling me that I couldn't adopt him. Even so, I knew I wanted to show him the same loyalty and love he had shown his owner in his time of need. Bruno needed ongoing specialist care to enjoy a nice quality of life into his senior years, and this is a big financial investment for the charity. I felt I needed to contribute, in my own small way.

I had shared his story with my family, and I could tell he had captured their hearts as much as mine, so as a family we decided to sponsor him. Sponsoring a dog can be a fantastic way to help Dogs Trust for those of us who cannot adopt or foster. Signing up for a monthly donation helps the charity look after their longer-term residents with medical issues. Many dogs need this support and you can find out how to help on their website.

Hello Bruno,
Hope you are well, and happy.
I LOVE to eat too, especially
sausages.
It is really cool being your
friend and I hope you
have a great Christmas.

Love
Adam x

TED
New beginnings

Happiness is a warm puppy.

CHARLES SHULTZ

Does everything happen for a reason? This is a concept that is hard to grasp or believe when you see so many dogs abandoned needlessly every day. It can be difficult, at times, to think in terms of everything happening for a reason, particularly during the difficult period when a dog enters a pound or a rescue centre. But it can be very comforting to think that there is a purpose to this, and that, through this sequence of events, maybe the perfect dog will meet the perfect owner and some magical healing will occur and a bond of unconditional love will grow.

I know that dogs have touched my heart with a knowing glance, a loving lick or even a cheeky nuzzle through a muzzle! Working with these dogs has taken me to a level of consciousness that is unlike anything else I have experienced. Our connection is often unspoken, and it feels unworldly. In truth, what I get from them is beyond words and I simply haven't been able to capture it on film, or indeed on paper. It transcends any normal feeling and is on another level of explanation – but my heart knows. Often it's with your heart that you know a dog is meant for you.

It is hard to understand that connection if you are not a dog owner or an animal lover, and I get that. However, regardless of whatever that special connection is, I am thankful for these little creatures and the wonderful gifts and lessons they have taught me. I feel blessed.

As it is with all things in life, you can't anticipate the impact a four-legged creature will have on you. Dash arrived into my life when I needed him. My heart was heavy, I was drowning in grief, and my new little puppy kept me afloat and helped me navigate through the grieving process until I reached safe waters. In a way, then, having this dog paved the way for the work I continue to do now with animals on TV. What may be more surprising is that many of my best friends are also working with Dogs Trust. They say your vibe attracts your tribe, and that's true for me.

Maybe there are no coincidences in life. When a dog comes into your world, it might be for a reason, a season, or even for the duration of a lifetime, whether it's short or long. I know the love of a puppy was central to my own healing and, much like how Dash came into my life, one day a friend told me about someone who wanted to rehome puppies … and that led to an outcome I hadn't anticipated.

A very close friend, 'T', was grieving the loss of her dear dad. He had endured a particularly cruel and long drawn-out illness and she was completely heartbroken. I could recognise the signs. Her story was all too familiar. It had pained me to watch her lovingly nurse her father through illness, much the same as I had done with my dad. In close parallel with my own story, T decided to leave a job she loved to take some time for herself after the bereavement.

I could see she was hurting, but I didn't know how I could help. Like any good friend, I tried to be there for her and often we wouldn't talk about anything in particular, just chat. It was during one of our little catch-ups that I told her all about Dogs Trust. She said she would love to help in any way she could, now that her work was freelance and she had a lot more free time on her hands.

For me, my work with the charity continues when the cameras stop rolling. I am a regular fixture at the centre and have been known to rope in the support of my friends. T is such a good person, so I knew her offer of help was heartfelt. We agreed to meet and have a tour of the rehoming facility. My intention was to show her around and talk about the far-reaching work that they did and look at how she could get involved. With her vast expertise in PR and marketing, I felt sure she could offer some assistance. Secretly, I was also hoping that maybe, just maybe, a dog would catch her eye.

T had never been to the centre before and I could see was overwhelmed by the sheer size of the facility and the massive number of dogs housed under one roof. As we wandered around, she grew quieter and was taking it all in. For me, it's very normal and I can see past the many dogs and their loud barks clamouring for attention. But I could see she was struggling a little to get her emotions under control. She remarked on how many fabulous dogs there were, and she was right. It had been a while since I had taken a full wander around the corridors, and there had been many new arrivals, both young and old.

Some of my pals had gone home, like Kelly and Cosmo, so I stopped to chat with the other carers, who enjoyed telling me the happy tales. Sadly, some dogs were still there, like Claude, but I enjoyed stealing a moment to give them a little cuddle. The sight of so many types of dogs, big, small, young and old, can be a lot to take in. Some barked to say hello and some jumped up, staring at us with pleading eyes to get attention. I watched my friend stare around, wide-eyed, obviously taken aback by the size of the operation, and the reality of these dogs' lives.

I knew what she was feeling, so I said to her quietly: 'I know it is absolutely overwhelming, and I wished I could save every one of them too.' But she was having a different reaction – she was angry, despising the irresponsible humans who had put the dogs there. I had to agree, because at times I felt that way, too. But I told her that for now they were safe and getting the best care possible, as well as the best chance at finding a loving home.

As we continued our tour, T started to chat to different canine carers about different dogs. As she heard each story, she was drawn in and I could see the transformation come over her. She was wondering if she could give a dog a home.

We had seen almost all of the facility when I asked if we could go into whelping, where the new mums and puppies were housed. We walked down the aisle of kennels and that's when she spotted him, surrounded by his brothers and sisters. He seemed to like his own space – this beautiful puppy, with the most unusual coat, was enjoying his comfort, as he lay on his back, legs akimbo, taking up the entire soft bed while most of his siblings lay on the ground beside him.

The noise of our arrival woke him from his sleep and, without moving his body, he looked up and stared at us. He was part of an adorable litter of large, gangly, sweet-looking doggies, but he had most soulful eyes. T was immediately drawn to him and his littermates. I looked for the mum, but it seemed they had come in from a pound – very young with no mum. I immediately asked about them, and if he had a name yet. He didn't on paper, but soon he would be lovingly called 'Ted'.

Any feelings T might have been experiencing of stress, grief or even anger seemed to dissipate and all I could hear her say was, 'Awwwwww! Look at them! And would you look at that stunner staring at me.'

I have said so many times that even when I am having one of my worst days, I can look into the face of a puppy and suddenly all is right with the world again. It is a combination of those puppy dog eyes, the cute little nose and soft fur that melts even the coldest heart. It never fails to make people feel better. It is fair to say that the love hormone, oxytocin, was undeniably in the air between T and Ted. I took out my phone and took a picture, declaring to my good pal that I wanted to remember the moment they fell in love at first sight!

We all laughed, but T wasn't protesting. I joked with her then, saying, 'I have seen that look of love before. At your wedding to G!' (Yes, her husband is Gary, so they are G&T.) And soon, Ted would be added to their cocktail of love. It was a love she shared with the little puppy, I could see that clearly – an undeniable connection when they looked into each other's eyes, and something instantly changed.

They say the eyes are the windows to the soul. Well,

Ted's eyes radiated beauty and pure love. Watching them from a distance, I felt I was witnessing the healing power of dogs. I knew in that moment she would adopt him. 'Can we take him now?' she asked beseechingly. 'I could put him in my handbag!'

After a long time and much discussion about when puppies are ready for adoption, we finished our tour. This dog had crawled under her skin and somehow switched the light on in her heart again. I remember she texted me that night and asked me to send the pictures I had taken, so she could show them to her husband.

We spoke more about Dogs Trust the next day and she told me she couldn't stop thinking about Ted, the unusual puppy with the beautiful eyes. He had already become special to her, but now she was feeling guilty: he was a puppy, maybe they should look for an older dog? She pointed out there were hundreds more dogs in the same tragic predicament all around the country, and she was feeling very emotional about the whole situation. Then she mentioned her dad. I wondered if perhaps she might be experiencing some displaced grief about her father. She was talking back and forth, getting upset, rationalizing, questioning herself: 'I can't stop thinking about this little puppy, and yet I feel maybe we should try to help an older dog. Do you think it's a wise decision to take on this puppy?'

The whole thing was causing her a lot of stress, so I spoke gently, reminding her I that often we don't choose our dog, they choose us. I reassured her that it wasn't anything she had to rush into. As with all adoptions, she should go to the centre with Gary, her husband, and meet the litter a few more times. If she still felt the same way about Ted after a few visits, then she could have a chat with the behaviour team.

I felt sure she would know what the right thing to do was, and I was content in the knowledge that she would get the very best advice and help from the rehoming team.

So G&T organised a visit and officially met the litter, but they only had eyes for one boy. After spending a little time petting and playing with the bouncy pup, they captured him on camera, and in their hearts they knew they wanted to adopt him. However, the head has to come into it too, so like any responsible potential adopter they went home to consider it further and to do some research about the mixed breed – he was a Saluki/Lurcher cross. But really, there was no doubt in their minds. They soon initiated the steps to adopt their little Ted.

It was a massive decision for them because they both had busy careers and enjoyed travelling a lot. They had family in the UK, in Australia and scattered around Ireland, so adopting this little puppy wasn't an entirely straightforward matter and would need careful planning. But they were willing to make the twelve-year-plus commitment to this puppy. It wasn't long before their 'plus one' joined them, and was named Ted.

I can't say what happened that day when T saw Ted, or why some people rescue certain animals over others, but I do believe that destiny has a little hand to play in everything.

Maybe it is all about timing? One thing for sure is that with his colourful personality and unique character, Ted is exactly what she needed and he couldn't have come at a more perfect time. Whenever I have a chance, I visit Ted at T's, and it is so obvious how secure, loved and happy he is. But, like any first-time dog owner, T wasn't always so sure. At first she worried about him constantly and needed reassurance that she was doing everything okay. She spent the first two weeks indoors with him, and once again it reminded me of Dash and the time when he somersaulted into my life with boundless puppy energy.

Also like Dash, when Ted first arrived, he was a little shy about going out for walks, but I told her that this was completely normal. I reminded her that he was a baby, that everything was brand new to him, and that Dash and I hadn't gone outside the house either in the first fortnight. In no time, though, the once-sedate, doe-eyed dog transformed into a happy, playful puppy, diving for the nearest squeaky toy and running with it in his mouth at great speed around the house, and not to mention the park! He found his confidence and now loves bringing them for a walk. And once Ted settled and found his feet, T forgot her fears and relaxed into her new role.

Gary and T really enjoyed those precious puppy-love days. Like most young fur babies, Ted had no manners at first so he needed lots of teaching and training. But T could forgive him anything, especially as Ted made up for any of his naughty, destructive puppy tendencies with tons of puppy energy and lots of love. Being a good fur baby mum, she enrolled Ted in puppy classes and after a few lessons she reliably informed me that he was a star student. I wasn't surprised. Ted is a very sweet, affectionate, beautiful pup and a joy to be around. With his distinctive colouring and beautifully fluffy ears, he always seems to catch the eye of many admirers on his walks, both human and canine!

In truth, he is in many ways like his parents. Generally, he loves people and can be quite the social butterfly when around other dogs, but he can also be a little socially awkward and shy away from people, to enjoy his own time and space. But one thing always shines through, and that's his gentle, loving soul. Ted wouldn't hurt any living thing and just wants harmony, happiness and lots of love, always. He has blossomed with his new family and it's so lovely to see. Life has changed completely for Gary and T.

We are not number one anymore, he takes centre stage and we love that he makes us get out and about together. We meet so many more people and are much fitter with all the walks but, most importantly, he has made us find a better version of ourselves. He is a four-legged fur child and he completes our family.

Some people don't understand the strong bonds people have with their dogs and might be inclined to say, 'Don't be so crazy, a dog isn't family, it is an animal.' I have even heard some people sigh when T chats about putting Ted in doggy day care if she's working away from home, or paying for a dog-sitter when they go out. Many people wouldn't even entertain the notion of paying money for such things. I know she, too, has heard the undertones of their comments, implying, not-so-subtly, that this type of love should only be displayed towards people, namely children. But I understand it because it's just like my relationship with Dash – he is family! Ted is her number one priority and she loves him with all her heart. How can this bond not be equal to that of love for another person?

I know many are sceptical, but in fact, even science agrees that it is the same bond. Evidence published in the journal *Science* has suggested that dogs have used their lovable stare to win over the hearts of humans for thousands of years, and what's more, it can be proven. When interacting and exchanging gazes, both dogs and their owners experience rushes of the love hormone oxytocin, which is triggered by the eye contact.

I saw the 'love moment' with my own eyes when T met Ted, and I have seen that special stare and instant connection many times. Moments like those help fuel my soul to continue to help rescue dogs in any small way I can, so they can find their soulmate.

I didn't change the world by volunteering at Dogs Trust and I can't save every dog, but for every dog like Ted, I'm pretty sure their world has changed forever and so have the lives of those around them. And they've most certainly changed for the better.

Name:	Mick
Breed:	Springer Spaniel crossbreed

Arrived to Dogs Trust:

Mick arrived at Dogs Trust from Offaly pound with a swollen knee that was causing him to walk abnormally.

Dogs Trust History:

Mick was x-rayed and it was discovered that he had two old fractures that had healed incorrectly so his right hind leg had to be amputated to stop causing him discomfort.

Mick was super friendly towards new people and actively sought interaction by pushing his cute nose into people's hands.

He was also friendly towards other dogs and liked to play fetch.

Type of Home Required:

Children aged 5+

A secure garden is needed for this lively boy.

A loving family to help him recover from his operation.

MICK
Forever friends and forever homes

Dogs are our link to paradise. They don't know evil or jealousy or discontent. To sit with a dog on a hillside on a glorious afternoon is to be back in Eden, where doing nothing was not boring – it was peace.

MILAN KUNDERA

It is human nature to hold onto to past hurts, betrayals, abuse and traumas. We find it hard to release negative experiences and let go of our past. Too often we allow our past to dominate the present and dictate what's possible for our future. Dogs are different – they don't limit themselves in the same way. When I think about some of the things the Dogs Trust dogs have experienced, I am in awe of how they can trust humans again. But they seem to be able to take each moment for what it is and live in the present.

This has been a great lesson for me. Whenever I begin to dwell on my own worries, I now quickly remind myself to be more like my four-legged friends and take a dog's attitude to life. I look to the many dogs I've met in my life for inspiration during hard times, or when I feel my own pain or fears are becoming too overwhelming.

During my time filming TV shows about rescue dogs that had been abandoned, neglected or physically abused, I have seen these dogs prevailing despite the most hopeless situations they have found themselves in. These animals choose not to be the victims; they choose to take one step at a time in the present moment.

On the first day of filming the new series of *Dog Tales*, I had an 'aha' moment of sorts. It was quite unexpected, and it happened when I looked into the eyes of a very sick dog. I felt like I was afforded his vision for a small moment in time, and in that brief glance I could feel his optimism, he seemed open to all possibilities, despite appearances.

There is an old legend that I have read, an adaptation of the story about Adam and Eve in the Garden of Eden. It says that God allowed Adam to name all the plants and animals, as it says in scripture, but (here's the legend part) there was a small creature following God and Adam through the Garden and as they got to the end, the creature got their attention and spoke up: 'You have run out of names. There's not one left for me.' God looked down and smiled at the little animal. 'I have saved the best for last', he explained. 'I've turned my own name back-to-front, and called you dog.' I know this is just a story, but in that moment, looking at that sick dog, I felt like I had heard a whisper from heaven saying: Have hope – miracles do exist.

I met Springer Spaniel Mick immediately after he had just undergone surgery to have his leg amputated. My first job was to help the team on a vet run with another little dog called Louis, who also had a very sad past as he was a retired research facility Beagle. Louis had come into Dogs Trust in recent weeks from a laboratory facility in Ireland that was downsizing and, along with many other ex-research facility Beagles, the centre had taken them into their care and worked to find them all new homes. This little dog, Louis, wasn't walking and his carers were very worried. Naturally, because of where he came from, he was a nervous soul and everything seemed new to him. He obviously hadn't been exposed to the normal day-to-day things that most dogs do, like walking and running free. After a number of days of refusing to walk, there was a fear he might have an underlying health condition, so he was brought to an external vet for an x-ray. I was the carer chosen to accompany him on his vet visit. While it was Louis who brought me to the vet that day, it was Mick's story in the vet suite that caught my attention.

Louis was sedated for his procedure, so I had some time to pass waiting around for him to wake up. It was then that I overheard the team talking about the remarkable recovery of Mick, and how successful his operation had been. I had heard of Mick and knew he was also a referral from Dogs Trust, so naturally I felt nosey about him and was interested to find out more. I asked some questions and found out that

Mick had been a recent arrival at the centre. He had been rescued from a pound and although he was very young, aged at around one or two, he seemed to be in severe pain and discomfort and was walking with a limp. It was believed he might have an old injury or fracture to his hind leg that hadn't healed because it wasn't treated at the time. Nobody could be sure how this very young dog had received such a serious injury.

After extensive medical assessments and exploring all possible treatments, a decision was made to refer him to a specialist at Botanic Vets. The unfortunate conclusion the medical team had reached was that Mick would have to have the leg amputated. So that's what was happening when I stumbled upon his name and starting asking about him.

My first meeting with Mick will forever serve as a reminder to me to embrace life one step at a time. On hearing his story, I was filled with sadness at what he had been through, and without even meeting him I already felt a huge sense of pity for this dog. I felt his surgery and amptuation would hinder any chance he would have of living a healthy, happy life and I mourned for his lost future. The poor dog, everything was ruined for him – that's what I was thinking. How wrong I was!

I asked the specialist vet if I could meet Mick when she had to next examine him. I was told he was in the recovery room in the vet suite, so we made our way there, where I expected to find him lying down, almost paralyzed by the loss of a limb. My presumptions about little Mick were all to be proven wrong. I had notions of his limitations now with only three legs, but Mick clearly didn't.

He tried to get up, and quickly noticed something was a little different, but his eagerness and curiosity to meet us kept him moving along. He was determined, and he managed it, walking in a slightly awkward but defiant way, like a little baby taking those first milestone steps of independence. He managed to walk over to the vet, who did his post-operative check-up and confirmed this was the best possible outcome post-surgery; Mick was sprightly and alert, all good indications that he was well in himself.

His zest for life and desire to walk were immediately obvious to everyone. Even though he had tubes coming out of his wound, he was wagging his tail and delighted to see new faces.

We settled him into a comfortable kennel, and I sat on the floor quietly chatting to him. I looked into his eyes and I began to say things like, 'you're okay', 'well done', 'what a great boy', 'don't worry' … and I honestly felt he was looking back at me and saying, 'Don't worry about me, what about you? You only have two legs!'

In that moment I was reminded that, as humans, we tend to have trouble looking beyond the physical. I was feeling sorry for Mick, but that was me projecting my human feelings onto him. Dogs don't need our pity, they need our support and love. There was something about Mick that taught me this valuable lesson. He had spirit, and so much personality that I felt sure nothing was going to get him down. From that first glance I was invested in his recovery. I asked if I could be involved in his care, and was delighted when this was agreed by Cat.

Mick was the dog who surprised us all. He recovered very fast, was out running free in the field a lot sooner than anyone had expected and kept constantly amazing the team with his miraculous healing. The first day I filmed with him, out on his first big run off lead, he started to jump up on the agility structures and I was a nervous wreck, thinking he might damage his good legs. I remember thinking, 'Oh Mick, mind yourself.' I was so worried something would happen to him, especially as I was the one in charge of his care. But, as always, Mick was a cheeky chappie and full of the joys of life – he was the fastest dog on legs, even it was only three, in the field that day.

He seemed not only to lift the spirits of the staff but also of the other dogs. All of the dogs loved playing with him when they met out on free runs, and he was often kennelled with shyer dogs to bring them on in confidence.

This dog, possibly more than any other I've met, lived in the present moment and enjoyed every second of his life. He didn't seem to be affected by his past, and he didn't worry about tomorrow. He wasn't affected by what people perceived to be the consequences of his situation that meant nothing to him. He just enjoyed the here and now. Being around Mick was a constant reminder that we cannot change our past or determine our future, but we can live right now, accept our circumstances and enjoy life to the max. Honestly, if I could bottle this dog's special 'energy', we wouldn't have any problems in the world. What I learned from Mick was the important lesson that nothing in our life can affect us as much as our own decisions about how we deal with whatever challenge faces us. As we decide, so it is.

The more time I spent with Mick, the more I felt that he saw losing his leg as a gift. He was now pain-free, with a new energy and appreciation for his life. He focused every fibre of his being on all he could do with three healthy, free limbs. He never for one second focused on what he had lost. That's the beauty of dogs! They don't bury hurts. They don't harbour resentment. They just 'are'. I urge you to take a lesson from this dog – living in the moment is what true balance and gratitude are all about.

Mick's dog tale worked out perfectly and, as always, I felt the perfect person and family found him. He was chosen once he was put on the rehoming wing, and his adoption went through smoothly. I was eager to find out what happened next, so I arranged a home visit with his new owners, who told me the extraordinary way they had chosen Mick.

The Goldin family had been grieving the loss of their last four-legged family member, and had discussed as a family the possibility of getting another rescue dog. Dogs Trust wasn't even opened or in operation in Ireland when they got their first dog, who had lived happily with them for over ten years. A chance meeting for mum Liz on Bray seafront with an old friend ended up steering them towards the charity.

They went for a visit without any pre-conceived ideas of what kind of dog they were looking for. The youngest of the family happened to see Mick, who was kennelled at the end of the rehoming centre with another very shy dog. At that time, Mick had four legs and was awaiting surgery in the coming days, and he was far from the chap he is now. He was a little quieter then, and not as mobile because he was still in constant pain. Something inexplicable happened – an instant knowing or connection between Liz's son, Fiachra, and Mick. They locked eyes as Fiachra passed by the kennel and without thinking he said to Mick, 'I will be back for you.' Fiachra described to me how he just felt like he had known Mick before, and he was confident that this dog would be his new little four-legged brother. He said he never doubted this for a second, although his parents weren't so sure.

They inquired about Mick, and were told he wasn't up for rehoming at that time. They remember it was Catherine who helped them on the day, and she said, 'If he is meant for you, he won't pass you by.' She was so right.

Weeks passed and they decided to call the centre to ask again about the dog they couldn't stop thinking about. They were told that, sadly, his situation had changed and he now had only three legs. For the Goldins, this came as a bit of a shock. They hadn't considered a dog with a recent amputation and they wanted time to consider if they could look after his health needs. When they chatted to Fiachra about the new situation with Mick, there was no hesitation or doubt for the young boy – he still wanted Mick. In fact, he said he felt elated. They immediately began the process of adopting the newest member of their family.

Seeing Fiachra and Mick together on Bray beach, looking so happy and content, made me absolutely believe this was somehow meant to be. It seemed like no coincidence that I was meeting them in Mick's favourite place – Bray beach – which was, of course, the very place where that chance meeting had occurred that led the family to Dogs Trust. It made me feel even more strongly that we find each other, our dogs and us, and there is something magical in that finding. I know it sounds crazy, but I also know that it's true.

Stories such as these are a great reminder that the best lessons in life can come from the most unexpected places. The greatest lesson to learn from dogs is to live in the moment. To be fully present.

What an incredible gift dogs are to all of humankind.

EPILOGUE
Paws for thought

They say dogs come into our lives to teach us about love, and leave to teach us about loss. For me, Dashy came into my life and healed my grieving heart when I was trying to make sense of my new world without my father in it. Even after death, our love for those close to us does not die. Death is a reality we must all face, however, even dogs. I'm afraid that loss is not my strong suit, but maybe there is a lesson to be learned in the completion of the circle of life.

Dash is in the latter part of his worldly days now. I have seen him thrive from puppy to adolescent dog to full-grown adult canine, and now to his geriatric older years. He is slowing down, and my heart knows there will come a day when he won't be with me anymore, and it brings me to tears just to think of what that will feel like.

I truly love my dog Dash. I have never met a human who would greet me as warmly after being gone for an hour or so. He is all love, from the top of his nose to the tip of his wagging tail – endless, wonderful love.

I want to say thank you from the bottom of my heart to Dash and all the special furry friends I have met along the way for teaching me to embrace my inner mutt! They encourage me to strive to become 'top dog' in my own life, to adopt a dog's-eye view and to take on some doggy attitude.

I have never met a dog that had a master plan for their life, but they have plenty of lessons to bestow nonetheless. I am reminded of what Dash has taught me: to greet the ones I love with excitement and joy every time I see them, and to to be a loyal companion, loving unconditionally without judgment or measure.

Worrying about his advancing years is not truly embracing my inner Dash. Thinking of my own feelings is a selfish human act, and it isn't very dog-like. But then I am reminded of what he has taught me, which is that love is not selfish. Instead of feeling sad, I wipe the tears that are pouring from my eyes and think of everything I have learned from this special Labrador Retriever who saved me.

Our reward for being their masters is unconditional love and loyalty. Without dogs in my world, I would be a completely different person. So I embrace my inner dog and find joy in the little things in life — like the waves at the beach, or a run in the long grass. And, like them, I persist in the belief that no matter what age I am, I can always learn something new!

I wonder what the words of a dog would be for all of humankind, with so much pain in the world. I am sure there is something to learn from man's best friend and how they devote themselves so lovingly and loyally to us.

My constant companion sits beside me as I write every day, and sometimes I just sit and watch him as he rests and takes in the sounds around him. There's a huge focus on mindfulness and meditating in today's society, but I wonder if Dash has being doing this for years and I never saw it before? All I know is that when I am feeling stressed or overwhelmed, I take some Dash time – we find a quiet space and sit in silence, and it's so wonderful. It gives me the chance to think my thoughts through and it clears my cluttered mind. Who knows what our dogs are thinking? But they do seem to enjoy the quiet silence. Maybe as well as unconditional love, they can teach us about self-love too. Consciously taking some quiet time for ourselves can be calming, but it can also be a gesture of self-love. And if we can't love ourselves, who can we love?

Anyone who has ever enjoyed the special bond that owning a dog brings knows that no matter what life can throw at us, the sickness, the sorrows, the losses, the doubts or even life's abundance and radiant health, a dog is life's perfect prescription for constant love and caring. Once those four paws, or three in some cases, are around you, you are never alone or unloved. In a world of so much uncertainly, there is something very powerful in knowing that. Everything feels better when you are around your constant and caring companion. If you don't believe me, trust science.

Numerous studies have documented astonishingly powerful effects the interactions with dogs have had on humans. For example, stroking a dog has been shown to boost the immune system. Now researchers can explain the source of our companion animals' healing powers: it turns out that our pets profoundly change the biochemistry of our brains.

When we look into the eyes of our dog, the level of oxytocin in our brain rises. Oxytocin isn't known as the cuddle chemical for nothing! This same powerful chemical is released when a mother gives birth, leading her to bond fiercely with her newborn. Oxytocin causes a surge of physiological changes: it is proven it can slow heart rate and breathing, lower blood pressure and inhibit the production of stress hormones, thereby creating a profound sense of calm, comfort and focus. These conditions are critical to forming close social relationships – whether with a child, a life partner or a dog.

A large study conducted by the University of Missouri, USA, documented that petting dogs also caused a spike in serotonin levels. Serotonin is the neurotransmitter that most antidepressants attempt to elevate. The Missouri study's lead author, Dr Rebecca Johnson, states that 'we can help animal-assisted therapy become a medically accepted intervention'.

Taking all that into account, it's no wonder there are so many pet-assisted therapies helping so many in our society. I, for one, know with certainty that being around Dash and my four-legged friends in Dogs Trust has helped me with my own pains and losses. I can vouch for the love of a good dog – it has a powerfully healing effect. The good news is that these feelings can be mutual, too. We affect our dogs as well, and the same physiological changes can be seen in our pets as have been found in humans.

So think of this: by taking a dog from an animal charity like Dogs Trust, you already know you rescue two dogs – not just the one who comes home to be part of your family, but also the one who gets to take his place. And you know that your dog is going to bring you love, laughter and lightness. So really, rescuing a dog is a win–win situation.

It is often said you can't buy love, but I have witnessed people who have rescued it. But ask yourself this … who is really rescuing whom?

PART 3

Advice from Dogs Trust

OFFERING A DOG A FOREVER HOME

Why buy a dog or puppy when there are thousands of lovely unwanted and abandoned dogs at dog rescue centres and pounds all around Ireland, through no fault of their own? Dogs Trust usually has up to 200 dogs and puppies of all shapes and sizes in their rehoming centre in Finglas, all patiently waiting for their forever homes. Here are some reasons to adopt:

- it's incredibly rewarding
- you are giving a dog a second chance in life
- you are creating kennel space for another dog to be saved.

Think carefully about what kind of dog will suit your lifestyle and ask yourself the following questions:

- Is your home suitable for a dog?
- Do you have time to meet a dog's daily exercise and affection needs?
- Are there basic training classes or doggy day care centres in your area?
- Do you have family or friends that could help you look after your dog?

Dogs are a big financial commitment. Besides the cost of feeding them, they also require veterinary treatment. Dogs Trust strongly recommends that all adopters take out pet insurance.

When making your decision, factor in that your dog will require the following:

- his/her own comfortable bed
- food and water bowls
- toys
- treats
- regular treatment for fleas and worms
- annual vaccinations
- regular grooming.

If you work full-time but still really want a dog, there are lots of ways to ensure they are happy and looked after while you are at work.

- Before you get ready for work, taking your dog on a long walk then giving it a tasty chew stick before you leave will help your dog to become calm and relaxed.
- If you live close by, you can come home from work at lunch to spend time with your dog.
- Do you work in a dog-friendly work place that allows you to bring your dog to work with you?
- Is there be a doggie day care facility in your area?
- Do you have a friend or relative that you can either leave your dog with while you are at work or who will come to your house at lunch to spend time with your dog.
- Is there a dog walker in your area you can pay to walk your dog while you are at work, to break up his/her day?

Visiting Dogs Trust

When you visit Dogs Trust, the rehoming unit staff will ask you all about your home and your lifestyle, in order to help find the perfect dog for you! If you decide to adopt a dog, a member of the rehoming team will pop out to visit your home to ensure it is suitable for the dog you have chosen and to meet any other animals you may have to make sure they will get on together. The adoption fee is only €130 and every dog is:

- microchipped
- vaccinated
- vet checked
- neutered or spayed.

You will also receive the following:

- six weeks' free pet insurance
- A starter bag of food
- A collar and a lead
- Pre-adoption talk
- Free behaviour advice for the rest of your dog's life.

ADOPTING A PUPPY

It's true, puppies are always the star attraction at Dogs Trust and it can be the best feeling in the world giving a puppy a loving home. However, it is important to remember that it will be almost like having a little baby in the house; they need a lot of time, care and attention. Like an infant, puppies can sleep for the majority of the day, but you'd better be prepared for the burst of energy when they wake up. Puppies are lovely, but can be a lot of really hard work. Be prepared for months of disruption, chaos and mess – puppies aren't really for the seriously house-proud! Owning a puppy can be a real joy, but it's also a serious responsibility to lay the correct groundwork so that you end up with the dog of your dreams.

Choosing a breed

It is essential to choose a breed that will best suit your circumstances. Research the different breeds by reading books and gain as much information as possible before making your choice.

Think about your lifestyle, size of home, facilities for exercise and time available. Speak to other dog owners for their advice and experiences. Consider both the physical and mental needs of the breed you have chosen.

Once you have chosen your puppy, it is important to make plans for the transition to your home. This will help reduce any extra stress caused by new surroundings and give your puppy the best start in a new life. Here are some basic guidelines for you to follow.

Preparation

* Decide on a name for your new puppy. This will be one of the first things they will learn.
* Decide where your new puppy is going to sleep and have a suitable bed ready with a blanket or an old jumper. Many people choose to place the bed in the kitchen, where the floor is easy to clean and the area is free from draughts, and not near a busy doorway/entrance hall.
* Ensure you have all the necessary equipment, such as a feeding bowl, a water bowl, a couple of safe toys and suitable grooming equipment for the coat type. You will be given a lead, collar, temporary name tag and small supply of food when you collect your puppy from Dogs Trust.
* Ensure the home environment is safe. 'Puppy proofing' is wise to avoid any unnecessary accidents. Remove anything that you would not wish to be chewed, particularly electrical flexes, and ensure that garden fencing and gates are secure.

Bringing your puppy home

When you collect your puppy, it is best if two people can make the journey so someone can hold the puppy in the car. It is a good idea to bring some old towels or newspaper in case your puppy gets car sick.

Your puppy will be slightly confused and bewildered when they first arrive to your home, so try not to overwhelm them. Avoid the temptation to invite friends and family over until they have settled in and spent at least a few days in your home.

Let him explore the areas of the house they can access and show them their bed and food and water bowls. There are dog appeasing pheromones available to buy from your vet, which are calming to dogs and puppies. They are available in collar, spray and plug-in form, and will really help your puppy to settle.

Place a suitable collar on your puppy and allow him to get used to it. Fasten it up, but leave enough room that you can fit two fingers underneath to make sure it's not too tight. Adjust it as your puppy grows.

Even if your puppy is a little 'stinky', avoid the urge to give him a bath until they have settled in as it will be too overwhelming for him. You can use a damp towel if they are particularly smelly.

Ensure all children in the house understand that the puppy is not a toy and that they need to sleep undisturbed and handled gently.

Socialisation

Socialisation means getting your puppy used to sights, sounds and people in a positive way so that they grow up to be a confident, happy and well-rounded dog! Although it is very important to begin the process of socialising your puppy as soon as possible, you must ensure that they arent exposed to potentially fatal canine diseases and is fully vaccinated before they go on walks.

You can, however, carry him around to see people, experience traffic, public transport or to meet other dogs you know have been fully vaccinated. Be careful not to let him touch the ground, especially in areas like the park, where unvaccinated dogs may have been.

Although the term might be new to you, socialisation is quite simple really. It essentially involves letting your puppy experience new things and praising good, calm behaviour. **Here are some examples:**

- Stand with your puppy beside the road (start at a distance from a quiet road) and let him watch and listen as cars go by. If they sit with you calmly, tell him he's a good boy and give him a treat.
- Ask a friendly person to speak to and pet your puppy gently under his chin. If your puppy is happy, doesn't nip at the stranger's fingers or bark, then praise him and ask the stranger to give your puppy a treat.
- Let him meet a friend's vaccinated, well-behaved

adult dog in your garden on a regular basis. Supervise them closely and watch how your puppy learns their doggy social skills. Praise your puppy for gentle play and friendliness towards the other dog – remember that it is okay for an older dog to tell a puppy off (without hurting the puppy) if they bite too hard or forgets his manners!

- Teach your puppy to be gentle, calm and obedient, even in exciting circumstances – especially around children.

There are some **'don'ts'** when it comes to socialisation too:

- You don't want to encourage your puppy to be scared, so if your puppy shows a nervous reaction to anything new, remove them from what is scaring him until they seem okay and then try again later at a slower pace.
- Don't let your puppy play with other dogs or get too boisterous as this can encourage them to greet other dogs inappropriately as they gets older.
- Never allow your puppy to jump up at or nip the hands of people they meet. Teach them to sit calmly beside you or in your arms while they are being petted.
- Don't try to expose them to too many new things in one day, or you could overwhelm them and do more damage than good. Try to experience no more than three new things a day.

ADOPTING AN OLD AGE DOG

Having a bouncy, happy, playful puppy is a very enjoyable experience, but it is also a big commitment, demanding much of your time, money and care. Remember, a puppy will grow into a dog and will be with you for many years to come – an average of thirteen years!

Old age dogs (OADs) are often overlooked in favour of puppies, but do remember that they, too, are in the care of Dogs Trust through no fault of their own. It may be that their previous owner moved to accommodation that did not allow dogs, or emigrated, or perhaps simply abandoned the dog because they were not able for the responsibility of dog ownership. So, please, don't discount adopting an adult dog.

Senior dogs often find themselves looking for a new home in their twilight years and can often be overlooked due to their age. Dogs over the age of seven are considered by some to be old, but this depends a lot on the breed. The 'average' life expectancy of a dog is thirteen years, but smaller breeds generally tend to live longer than larger breeds.

You may think that older dogs are more likely to have been diagnosed with health problems and worry about the cost implications of rehoming an older dog. In some circumstances, Dogs Trust may offer financial support for identified conditions, so please don't let this put you off.

You might also be thinking that it would be too upsetting to adopt an older dog, as they may not have many years left. Although it is true that older dogs have less time left, by adopting one, you have the power and the privilege to make that dog's last few months or years the happiest of their entire life. You will also value the time you spend with your dog more because that time is so precious. There really is nothing more rewarding than giving a dog the retirement home they so deserve.

Advantages of an OAD

- You don't have to adopt a puppy to form an amazing bond with a dog. Dogs who have lost their previous owner(s) can be more likely to form strong attachments to the new person in their life, especially if that person shows them lots of love and affection.
- When rehoming an older dog, what you see is what you get because his size and personality have already been shaped. There is no wondering about how big they will get, or if they will be calm or giddy, affectionate or silly. It's all there, right in front of you.
- Older dogs can generally have the run of the house because, unlike their younger counterparts, they are less likely to get up to mischief or chew on your

prized possessions. They also tend to have better manners and most are already house-trained.

- Senior dogs are less demanding, often calmer and more relaxing to be around and most require less exercise, being content to snooze most of the day away after their walk.

- Contrary to popular belief, you can teach an old dog new tricks! Older dogs still enjoy mental stimulation and training, as long as it is not too physically strenuous.

- There are plenty of dogs of all shapes and sizes, as well as different ages, at Dogs Trust. If you've been thinking of adding a dog to your family, pop in and have a chat with their experienced adoption team. Hopefully you'll be a #specialsomeone (our new campaign) to one of their dogs and give them a happy life.

Looking after your older dog

Old age brings many changes, some sudden, others gradual, and you will need to be on the lookout for those that signal problems. By preparing for your dog's later years, you can really enhance the quality of life that they deserve.

Older dogs may struggle with their sight and hearing. Your dog's eyes may appear cloudy, which could mean that they have cataracts. Seek veterinary advice on this.

Most dogs adjust to failing sight, since it is usually a gradual process. Try to avoid moving the furniture in your house or leaving objects in his way.

Keep him on the lead during exercise, especially near roads, as your dog may lose the ability to hear certain sounds.

You will also need to pay particular attention to the condition of his teeth and the length of his nails. His nails may be less worn as his walks become shorter.

If your dog hasn't already been neutered, there may still be benefits in doing so at an older age. Seek veterinary advice on this.

Your dog's coat may change in condition. Daily grooming will be good for his coat, and this is also a great opportunity to check him over for any lumps or bumps that may indicate a problem. Twice yearly veterinary check-ups are essential for an ageing dog.

To help your dog remain mentally active, try to introduce new and interesting aspects into his routine. Make plenty of time for games and interaction with him.

Feeding and diet

As they become less active, older dogs can be prone to putting on weight, but switching to a complete senior food, which may be lower in protein or fat, will help keep that extra weight off. If your older dog suffers from neck or back pain, raising his food and water bowls off the ground will help reduce discomfort.

Exercising older dogs

Older dogs can become less energetic and sleep more, so while out on walks, try to let your dog set the pace. It is usually better to go for frequent short walks instead of one long one. Your dog may not want to go on long hikes as they get older, but it is still important to exercise him so that they stay fit, gets enough mental stimulation and keeps his joints mobile. They may show signs of joint stiffness in the morning or after exercise, so ensure they have a comfy bed to sleep on and seek veterinary advice on managing this, as there are lots of treatments available for joint issues! You may want to provide a dog ramp to help them navigate the stairs and for accessing your car too, and these can be found online and in many pet shops.

LOST DOGS

Losing a dog is every owner's nightmare. No matter how careful you are, accidents happen and dogs can escape from your home, slip off their lead or run off chasing a squirrel while you are out walking. It can be very upsetting and stressful, so it's important to know who to call and what to do to have the best chance of being reunited quickly with your dog.

- As it is now a legal requirement, your dog should be microchipped. This means that if they are presented to a dog pound, animal welfare organisation or a veterinary practice, you will be contacted immediately.
- All dog owners must not only have their dogs microchipped but must also be in possession of a valid microchipping certificate, in order to be compliant with the law.
- Your dog should wear a collar and ID tag at all times so you can be quickly contacted in the event of them going missing. Dogs Trust recommends that your surname and contact numbers are on the ID tag.
- If your dog strays, share their photograph and your contact details locally and online to spread the word. Make contact with your local dog pound, animal

welfare groups and local veterinary practices to tell them about your lost pet.

- If your dog is already microchipped, make sure the correct details are registered against the chip and apply for your certificate online via www.fido.ie. If you do not have a record of your dog's microchip number, your local veterinary practice will scan your dog for you and let you know the microchip number.

I CAN'T COMMIT TO A DOG, BUT I WANT TO HELP

Dogs Trust has an amazing team of dedicated canine carers at their rehoming centre, but with so many dogs and puppies to look after, extra pairs of hands are always greatly appreciated! There are many ways you can help out – look at the list below and see if something there suits you, then get involved!

Volunteering

Volunteers help in many aspects of Dogs Trust's vital and lifesaving work, whether it is helping at their events, giving a dog waiting for its new home some extra love and attention, or ensuring the rehoming centre looks welcoming and attractive to visitors and potential adopters. Every role is so important to the dogs and their success in finding their forever home. This is the role I played in my time at the charity and I can wholeheartedly recommend it. The staff are wonderful, the centre is an eye-opener and the dogs are a complete and utter joy. I found it life-changing, and I'm so glad I took the plunge and became a volunteer.

Dogs Trust literally has a job for every volunteer, such as helping with:

- administration
- dog walking
- kennel cuddles
- puppy socialisation
- gardening
- cleaning
- laundry
- home visits
- dog training
- maintenance
- fund raising.

Volunteers are an integral part of the Dogs Trust team, who could not achieve their mission without them. By volunteering at Dogs Trust, you could make a real difference to a dog's life. Remember, they love to hear from both individuals and corporate organisations. If you're interested, you can apply to volunteer at Dogs Trust via: www.dogstrust.ie

Fostering

Dogs Trust is always looking out for foster homes to help with the dogs in their care. Having fantastic foster-carers allows them to take in even more dogs in need. If you think the following sounds like you, please do get in touch:

- you have time to care for a puppy or adult dog
- you live within driving distance of the centre in Finglas
- you can commit to an average of eight weeks of care
- you don't mind what breed/age/size pup you take.

Usually Dogs Trust requires foster homes for puppies, but on occasion they will require foster-carers for adult dogs who are recovering from surgery and need a home to recuperate in. Dogs Trust will provide you with all the food, bedding and toys for your foster dog, and any additional support you may need during the dog's stay at your house. To apply to become a Dogs Trust foster-carer, download the puppy fostering form via their website at www.dogstrust.ie and e-mail it to: reception@dogstrust.ie.

Sponsoring a Dog

If you can't have a dog yourself or if you are searching for the perfect gift for a dog-loving friend or family member, why not sponsor a Dogs Trust dog? You'll be joining 4,436 other generous people who are happy to show they care – and Dogs Trust is most grateful that they do!

Dogs Trust finds homes for the vast majority of dogs in their care. However, some of the dogs can be more difficult to rehome due to behaviour or health issues. Since Dogs Trust never destroys a healthy dog, they promise to take care of these dogs for as long as it takes. So, to help them look after their longer-term residents, they ask the public to sponsor these special dogs by signing up for a monthly donation via direct debit. The donations raised go towards your chosen Sponsor Dog and all the other dogs in their care. You can sponsor a dog yourself or on behalf of someone else.

When amazing dog lovers like you sponsor a dog, Dogs Trust just loves to let you know how your dog is getting on. You will receive letters, cards and messages. It's the least they can do – after all, sponsorship helps their dogs to have warm beds to sleep in, food to eat, walks and cuddles, and important things like medicine and vet care as well.

Simply visit www.dogstrust.ie and click on 'Sponsor a Dog'.

Donations

If you love dogs, but lead a very busy lifestyle and just don't have the time to foster or volunteer, perhaps you could help the dogs in Dogs Trust by providing some of the following items:

Dog training aids

- Hotdogs
- Packets of ham, chicken and lunch meat
- Blocks of cheese
- Soft cheese triangles
- Smooth peanut butter
- Pâté
- Fresh/frozen raw chicken
- Collars and harnesses

Dog dinners

- Tinned tuna/sardines
- Tinned dog meat
- Dry pasta
- Frozen vegetables

Dog chews

- Dental-type chew treats
- Natural rawhide

Dog bedding

- Duvets (not the feathered variety – the dogs like to make these into 'snow'!)
- Sheets and blankets
- Bath mats and towels
- Pet carriers
- Dog crates (with bases)

Dog toys

- Teddies are like gold, we love to receive them!
- Interactive toys
- Squeaky toys
- Old baby toys, such as play mats and plastic garden toys.

FREQUENTLY ASKED DOG QUESTIONS

Q. How long should my dog spend sleeping?

A. While it differs from dog to dog, a normal, healthy adult dog will sleep or doze in many sessions across the day and night, and this can add up to 12–14 hours over a 24-hour period.

Q. How often should my dog be vaccinated?

A. Puppies should be vaccinated at between six and nine weeks of age, and then again at ten to twelve weeks. They will become fully protected two weeks after the second vaccination. Regular 'booster' vaccinations are then necessary to keep the dog's immunity levels high enough to protect him against disease throughout his life. Your vet will advise you on how often your pet needs to be vaccinated.

Q. Why does my dog bark at the postman?

A. Look at this situation from your dog's point of view. While relaxing or sleeping in his home, they are startled by the gate, letterbox or even the doorbell and a man or woman in uniform. They act by 'shouting', otherwise known as barking, at the intruder and, lo and behold, they leave! As this happens regularly, the dog thinks that it is his barking that is getting the postman to leave and therefore repeats the behaviour.

Q. Can my dog eat that?

Safe for your dog			
✓ Strawberries	✓ Pineapples	✓ Blueberries	✓ Kiwis
✓ Broccoli	✓ Bananas	✓ Peas	✓ Oranges
✓ Cucumber	✓ Carrots	✓ Cauliflower	✓ Potatoes

Not safe for your dog			
✗ Yeast	✗ Alcohol	✗ Chocolate	✗ Cherries
✗ Grapes	✗ Avocados	✗ Raisins	✗ Onions
✗ Caffeine	✗ Artificial sweetener	✗ Macadamia nuts	✗ Garlic

Q. Is it okay to leave my dog unattended?

Dogs have been selectively bred for thousands of years to be very social animals and, as a rule, are most content when they are with their family and with other canines. Because they form such strong bonds, dogs can become anxious when their owners leave the house. They can also become bored, especially if left for long periods, and this can lead to all sorts of mischief, destructive behaviours, barking and/or howling. Accordingly, Dogs Trust generally recommends that dogs are not alone for more than four hours at a time.

HOW TO BE DOG SMART

Pulling his tail, sitting on him, disturbing his sleep and kissing his nose are just some of the unhelpful ways children can act around dogs, according to a survey released by Dogs Trust in 2017. The charity urges parents never to leave a child alone with any dog as part of its groundbreaking 'Be Dog Smart' dog safety campaign. This is a free nationwide education program to teach all family members how to stay safe around dogs, whether in the home or out and about.

How to safely approach a dog

- When approaching a new dog (and only when the owner is present), walk up to the owner and ask permission to rub the dog. Do not walk straight up to the dog and never run towards, or away from, the dog.
- Stay nice and calm when you approach. Dogs can get overexcited by lots of activity and loud noises, and we don't want them to jump up or get a fright!
- If the owner gives permission, curl your fingers into a ball and hold it down towards the dog. Let the dog come to you and sniff your hand. We call this our 'safe hand'.
- Ask the owner where the dog likes to be rubbed and then gently stroke the dog there.

- If a dog is by themselves, either running loose or tied up outside a shop, you should never attempt to pet them. If a dog is tied up, and isn't used to children, they have nowhere to run if they get a fright.
- You should always ask the owner, not a stranger, before you pet a dog.

What to do if you are scared of a dog

- If approached by a dog and you feel scared, stand still and upright. Bring your arms into an 'X' across your chest, keeping your hands up and away from the dog. We call this the 'X Factor'!
- Don't look at or talk to the dog. Turn your head up towards the sky and don't give them any attention at all.
- Walk away calmly and slowly (don't run), keeping your arms crossed in an 'X'. Ignore the dog and don't turn back to see where they are.
- Walk indoors or towards someone who can help you – not a stranger.
- Never try to run away from a dog – they love to chase things! If we run, the dog might think we're playing a game with them and could chase us or jump up.
- When riding a bike, get off and use the bike as a barrier between you and the dog. Walk calmly indoors or find someone you know who can help.

- If a dog jumps up at you, do the X Factor. Keep your hands up and cross them over your chest. Then turn to the side slightly.
- If you get knocked over by a jumping dog, curl up into a ball on the ground covering your head and your neck with your arms. Wait for an adult to help or for the dog to go away.

For more information on the Be Dog Smart campaign, you can visit www.bedogsmart.ie where you can book a workshop for your school or community with your local Education and Community Officer and download the Be Dog Smart resources.

ACKNOWLEDGEMENTS

While there are probably dozens of people who deserve a big THANK YOU for helping make this book a reality, I want to acknowledge the countless big-hearted unsung heroes that fight for the welfare and protection of dogs day after day. I have been fortunate to work with many rescue organisations and I am in awe of their commitment and dedication. I want to thank most sincerely Suzie Carley and the amazing team at Dogs Trust for accepting me as part of their pack. I am so grateful to all the adopters who have allowed me to share their dog tales in this book, and, of course, to photographer Fran Veale for capturing the bond between the dogs and their owners so brilliantly.

I want to thank TV3, especially Ben Frow, Andrew Byrne and Lynda McQuaid for affording me the opportunity to make TV shows about animals, and not forgetting all the brilliant production teams I have worked with over the years.

Books, like dogs, can change your life, and none of my three books would have been written without my super editor, Sarah Liddy. This book was very close to my heart, and the expert team at Gill Books have supported me throughout the whole process and have made it so enjoyable to write, so thanks to Gill.

It was a pleasure to meet the author of one of my favourite dog books, *Marley and Me*. I cannot explain how overwhelmed with gratitude I am that John Grogan read and enjoyed my *Dog Tales*. From the bottom of my heart, thank you.

I have to give special mention to all my wonderful friends, too many to include here, but especially my best pal and PR queen Valerie Roe and my friend Vanessa Fox O'Loughlin for always being by my side, supporting my efforts. Always cheering me on are my biggest supporters, my wonderful husband David Torpey; my daughter Brooke; siblings Lavinia, Maria and Brian; and my mum Marie, who have all endured me living all things *Dog Tales* for months now. I am forever grateful and candles will be burning for you all in St Anne's church.

However, all of the above is really secondary to whom this book is dedicated too – wo(man's) best friend – dogs!

Most specifically, my dog Dash, who has loved and served me loyally for twelve years and has comforted me, protected me and given me unconditional love. The special bond between humans and dogs is as old as time and is one of the most durable friendships ever documented.

So as you read and reflect on these stories of love, hope, loyalty and loss, please take another look at your own four-legged friend, and give them an enormous big hug and shower them with endless love.

This book is dedicated to your dog and mine; and to all canines that have pawed their way into our hearts. After all, dogs make us better humans, and in this day and age that is something to cherish and celebrate.

So for all the dogs who have allowed me to gain their trust, and most especially for my dog Dash, from the bottom of my heart – thank you!

I think all dogs are deserving of a book in their honor. So to all our canine companions, these dogs' tales and this book are dedicated to you and it is written with love and gratitude.